THROUGH THE EYE OF THE NEEDLE

STORIES FOR WHOLE LANGUAGE LEARNING

HOLLY L. EUBANKS

ILLUSTRATED BY ANN C. CHAPIN

Dominie Press, Inc.

Publisher: Raymond Yuen
Project Editor: Liz Parker
Text Layout: Gary Hamada

© 1993 Dominie Press, Inc.
Reprinted 1994
Reprinted 1998

All rights reserved. No part of this publication may be reproduced or transmitted in any form or by any means without permission in writing from the publisher. Reproduction of any part of this book, through photocopy, recording, or any electronic or mechanical retrieval system, without the written permission of the publisher is an infringement of copyright law.

Published by

Dominie Press, Inc.
1949 Kellogg Avenue
Carlsbad, California 92008

ISBN 1-56270-047-2

Printed in U.S.A.
3 4 5 6 7 8 W 99 98

DEDICATION

Ann and Holly wish to recognize and express our gratitude to
the family and friends who helped with this project.

From Ann, thanks to my husband David,
who is wholly supportive of my pursuit of art.

To David (again) who sees unexpected things in pictures
(like a monkey instead of a hat), thereby reminding me that perception
is interactive; Vern for his meticulous wisdom about composition;
Allen, Dragon Lady, Holly, and Dad for their encouragement of my artistic
endeavors; Zuni for her friendship, teaching me organization, and the love of
Florida skies; my son Mykel for his valuable perspectives as a student;
Adam and Eve (pet snakes), and Purr and Squidget (pet cats)
for their modeling services.

From Holly, so much appreciation to our dad, who taught me to love
the spoken and written word; to my daughter Selene, for her inspiring exhuberance and sense of
humor; to my lifelong friend Carole Bergman who has listened patiently to countless revisions of
the stories; to my friend and colleague Sheri for her humor and encouragement; to Nadine for her
suggestions on maskmaking; and to Jan Vanderpool for working far
into the night to fix my computer.

A very special acknowledgement goes to Mr. David Pandy in Belize
who gave me the Bra' Anansi story over the phone;
and to Lloyd Pandy for translating it from the original Creole.

We are grateful to our publisher, Raymond Yuen, for giving us this forum;
and to our gifted editor, Liz Parker, for her tactful—
but always insightful—suggestions.

Finally, to all of the wide-eyed children who have listened
to these tales over the years, this is for you.

CONTENTS

1 Bra' Anansi and Bra' Tiger, *Belize* 1

2 Bra' Anansi and Bra' Tiger, Part II, *Belize* 10

3 The White Cat, *France* 19

4 The White Cat, Part II, *France* 30

5 Three Brothers, *Russia* 40

6 Three Brothers, Part II, *Russia* 50

7 Wassilissa the Beautiful, *Russia* 59

8 Wassilissa the Beautiful, Part II, *Russia* 68

9 The Ghost, the King, and the Sorcerer, *India* 78

10 The Ghost, the King, and the Sorcerer, Part II, *India* 87

11 Cap o'Rushes, *England* 96

12 Cap o'Rushes, Part II, *England* 107

BRA' ANANSI AND BRA' TIGER

ra'* Anansi was just an ordinary grey spider. He lived in the jungle with all the other animals. But for an ordinary little spider, he had one extraordinary talent. From a substance in his body, he could make his own ropes. These were not real ropes, but sticky, silky, thin threads. He would weave these back and forth into a beautiful web. The web was a trap. In it he caught flies and other small insects. These he ate. But being small made him easy prey for birds and other animals. So he thought about what he would do.

Bra' Tiger lived in the jungle. He was big, strong, feared by all other animals. Bra' Anansi thought it might be a good idea to become his friend.

Bra' Anansi called down from his web.

"Say there, Bra' Tiger. Do you know that there is a town at the edge of this jungle? I have been there. And I have seen the loveliest maidens that ever walked upon the face of the earth. Wouldn't you like to meet one of them?"

Bra' Tiger looked around. He could not see who was talking to him. "Look up. Look up here."

Bra' Anansi was busily spinning a web just above Bra' Tiger's ear. He did not seem to be the least bit afraid of the great cat.

* *Bra'* means *brother*.

Bra' Tiger went to the edge of the water and looked down.

"You say there are girls in this town?" Bra' Tiger was interested. "Pretty ones?"

"I could take you there now."

And they went.

Indeed, there were many lovely maidens in the village. But one above all was a stunning beauty. Both Bra' Anansi and Bra' Tiger spotted her at the same time. Both decided to court her. Each was determined to win her as his bride.

Bra' Anansi pretended to be tired. "Would you mind, Bra' Tiger, taking me on your back to the forest? It was such a long trip to town that I have grown weary. We will make plans to return another day."

Bra' Tiger agreed. But no sooner had they parted ways than Bra' Anansi turned around and went back to town. He went to the maiden's house and knocked loudly at the door. She let him in.

Once inside, Bra' Anansi wasted no time in declaring his affection for the girl. He composed poems, he sang her song after song, he tickled her cheek with his delicate feet. But she was not impressed.

"You are such a dear, Anansi," she said, "but you are just not my type. I'm afraid I just could not fall in love with someone with eight legs. Tiger is much prettier, much softer, much sleeker, much stronger. And besides, he is a much better fisherman than you are. I would never have to worry about being hungry with him at my side."

"Bra' Tiger is not such a good fisherman as all that," retorted Bra' Anansi. "I am a much better fisherman than he is."

"Oh?" questioned the girl. "Those are bold words. Is there any truth to them, or are you just bragging? Can you prove it?"

"Of course," said Bra' Anansi. "I'll be back tomorrow. Wait and see."

The next day Bra' Anansi was awake early. He scurried over to where Bra' Tiger lay sleeping and woke him up.

"Say there, Bra' Tiger, wake up! I have something to show you."

Bra' Tiger grunted. He was not pleased to have his sleep disturbed.

"Bra' Tiger! *Wake up!* I have found something wonderful! I want to show it to you."

"What is it?" snarled the tiger.

"I have found a treasure, to be sure. And because you are such a good friend I will share it with you alone."

The great cat was now wide awake. He eyed the spider suspiciously. "What treasure could you have found that I would want?"

"Come with me," said the spider.

He led the tiger deep into the jungle. At a spot tangled with vines and roots he stopped. "Look under there," he said.

The tiger pulled back the vines. There underneath was a very large well.

It was full to the brim with water, and large fish could be seen swimming just below the surface.

Bra' Tiger swished his tail with excitement. He leaned over the lip of the well and dipped his paw into the water. Out it came with a fat fish. Again the paw sliced through the water and yanked out a second fish. In no time there was a heap of fish lying on the ground beside the well. Bra' Tiger picked one of the biggest and began to eat it. While he wasn't looking, Bra' Anansi took one of the other fish and scraped off its scales. He dropped them into the water and they drifted to the bottom. The fish scales caught the rays of the sun and shone brightly. And because the water magnified them, they looked every bit like coins.

"Come here, Bra' Tiger," called the spider. "I want you to see something."

Bra' Tiger went to the edge of the water and looked down.

"Look at all that money," said the spider. "I want to get it. I want to take it to the girl in town. I'm sure she'd be very pleased to receive a gift like that."

Bra' Tiger did not say anything right away. At last he spoke. "Why don't you let me help you, Bra Anansi? That looks like a lot of money to carry. And you wouldn't be able to get it out of the well anyway."

"How would you get it?" asked the spider.

"Take one of these vines," answered the tiger. "Tie it around my waist. Lower me down into the well. I will get the money. When I am ready I will call to you. You will pull me back out."

The spider agreed. But as soon as the tiger was down in the well, Bra' Anansi pretened to lose his grip on the vine. He let it slip and the tiger hit the water with a splash!

"What have you done, Bra' Anansi?" sputtered Bra' Tiger. "You idiot! Get me out of here before I drown!"

"Oh, Bra' Tiger! I am so sorry! You were too heavy for me. I will get help."

And off scurried the spider—taking the fish with him! He took them straight to the door of the girl and knocked loudly.

She opened the door and saw the fish at her feet. "Oh, my, Bra' Anansi. You are a great fisherman!"

"Will you marry me, then?" asked the spider.

"Bra' Anansi, you are truly amazing. But I do not love you. Tiger is so strong, so handsome. And he has such beautiful white teeth. I do prefer him."

"Bra' Tiger has no teeth at all," snapped Bra' Anansi.

"What?" cried the girl. "No teeth? How can you prove that?"

"Just you wait. I'll be back."

End of Part I

THE WEBS WE WEAVE

Developing Creative Writing Skills

Before we write, we need to put our thoughts in order. What do we know about the topic? What ideas will we use in our writing? What do we write about first?
One way to organize our thoughts is with an outline. Another way is a web.

Work with a partner or a small group to organize your ideas. Study the web below. Notice how sub-groups branch out from other groups. Then choose one of the topics given or one of your own to make a web. Compare your web with your classmates' webs.

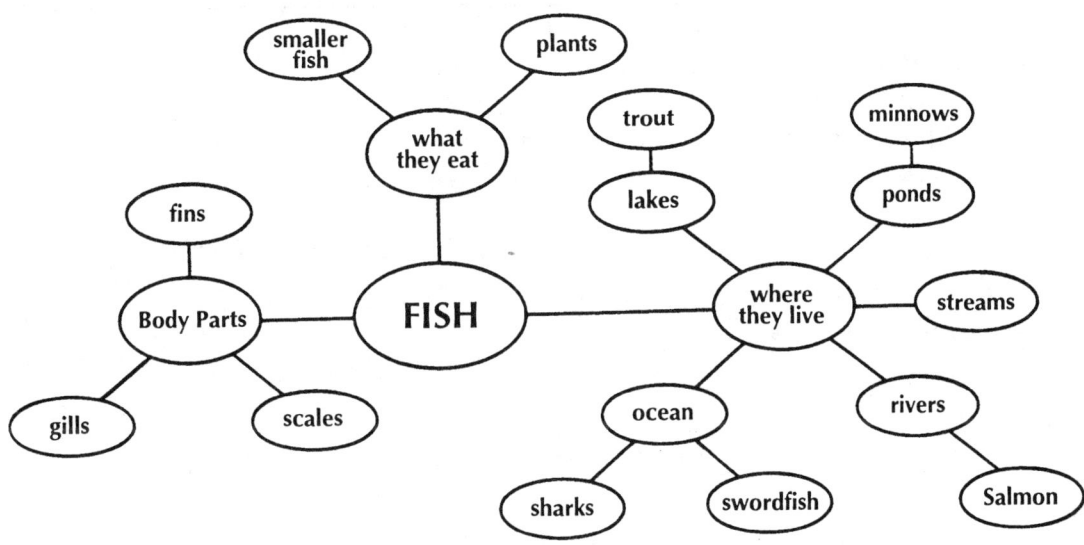

Choose one of the topics. Make a web.

spiders	lizards	insects
great cats	birds	jungles

STARS AND STRIPES FOREVER

Building Vocabulary

Tigers have beautiful orange and black stripes. Other things in nature have stripes, too. So do many things made by man.

Work with a partner or a team. List as many things with stripes as you can by name under each category below. Compare your list with your classmates' lists. One example is given.

Mammals	Animals of the Sea	Things We Wear
Reptiles	Animals That Fly	Things We Eat
Insects	Plants	Things Made of Plastic

Mammals – zebras
            raccoons
            house cats

THE SPIDER'S WEB

Bridging from the Story to Science

Different types of spiders spin different types of webs. Did you know there is a spider that spins a web between its feet? When an insect comes flying by, it shoots its web out like a butterfly net to trap its prey. See if you can find out the name of this spider.

For each spider below, find out what the web looks like. You will need to find a book on spiders or to work with a science teacher for help. Draw the web above the name of each spider.

Black Widow   Tarantula   Trap-door

Daddy long-legs   Brown recluse

NOTHING FISHY ABOUT IT

Building Vocabulary through Research

In the story, Bra' Anansi says that he is a better fisherman than Bra' Tiger. Did you know that there really is a spider that can catch fish? Find out the name of this spider.

Complete the information table for each spider. Then draw the spider. The first one is done for you.

	Description	Where It Lives	Poisonous/Not Poisonous to Man
Black Widow	Shiny black. Has a red, hourglass shaped spot on its abdomen. About 2.5 centimeters (1 inch) long.	United States and the Americas, New Zealand, Africa, most warm places of the world. Lives near dwellings and in dark places.	All species are poisonous to man.
tarantula			
trap-door			
daddy long-legs			
brown recluse			

WHAT DOES IT ALL MEAN?

Using Context Cues

When you read a new word in a story, you may not know what it means. Sometimes, you can use the sentences before and after to help you learn the meaning of the word.

Look at the underlined word in each sentence from the story. Use the story to help you choose the best definition of each word.

1. Bra' Anansi was just an <u>ordinary</u> grey spider.
   a. big
   b. old
   c. not special
   d. long-legged

2. But one above all was a <u>stunning</u> beauty.
   a. stupid
   b. brown-haired
   c. skinny
   d. amazing, wonderful

3. Both decided to <u>court</u> her.
   a. play tennis with
   b. try to win the love of
   c. kiss
   d. take to the king

4. It was such a long trip to town that I have grown <u>weary</u>.
   a. tired
   b. tall
   c. sick
   d. angry

5. Once inside, Bra' Anansi wasted no time in <u>declaring</u> his affection for the girl.
   a. telling
   b. crying
   c. screaming
   d. hoping

6. He <u>composed</u> poems.
   a. read
   b. listened to
   c. talked about
   d. wrote

7. He was not pleased to have his sleep <u>disturbed</u>.
   a. quiet
   b. noisy
   c. stopped
   d. bothered

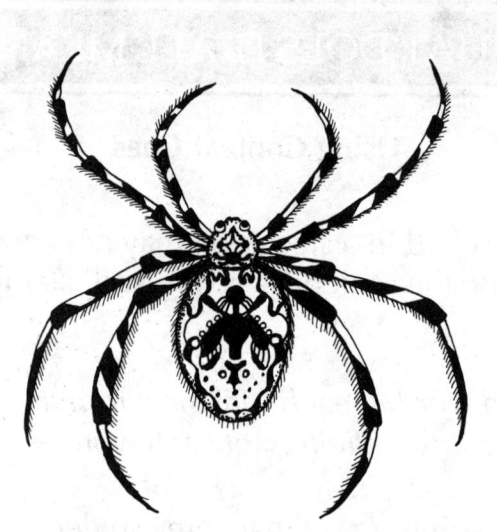

BRA' ANANSI AND BRA' TIGER, PART II

he spider scooted back into the jungle. He went straight to the well.

"Hold on, Bra' Tiger! I'll have you out in a minute!"

Bra' Anansi found a strong vine that was attached to a tree. He lowered it down into the well. Bra' Tiger climbed out.

The cat looked furious. He raised a paw and batted at the spider, but Bra' Anansi dropped a thread and sailed out of reach.

"Wait a minute, Bra' Tiger. This was not my fault. You're the one who suggested I lower you down into the well."

Bra' Tiger shook himself from head to tail. Water flew every which way.

"You miserable little bug. I ought to squash you! Where are my fish?"

"Someone stole them while I was gone," answered the spider.

Bra' Tiger flattened his ears back and swished his tail. "Get out of my way," he said. "I'm going home."

"Well, wait now, Bra' Tiger. I really feel badly about all this. Just to show you how sorry I am, let me give you a treat. I know where a mahmie apple tree is. It's full of ripe mahmie apples. I'll climb up in the tree and throw you the best fruit I can find."

Bra' Tiger did love mahmie apples. His mouth watered at the thought of them.

"All right, Bra' Anansi. As you say, this was not really your fault."

Once again Bra' Anansi led the way. He took the tiger to a giant mahmie apple tree. The big, brown, avocado-like fruit dangled invitingly. Bra' Anansi scampered up the tree, lickety-split.

"Okay, Bra' Tiger. I've found a big ripe one. Open your mouth wide, and I'll drop it down."

Bra' Tiger opened his mouth wide. Down shot the fruit. Plop! It fell right into his jaws.

Bra' Tiger licked his lips. "That was barely a bite, Bra' Anansi. Throw me another one."

Now, everyone knows that all mahmie apples look the same, ripe or not. Only by squeezing can you tell. Bra' Anansi scouted around until he found the biggest fruit on the tree. It was as hard as a rock.

"Open wide," he called.

Bra' Tiger opened his jaws wide. Down flew the fruit.

Crash! Crack! The fruit hit Tiger's jaw and knocked out all his front teeth!

"Oooo!" howled Bra' Tiger. "My teeth! My beautiful, sharp, white teeth! How could you do this to me?"

"It wasn't my fault, Bra' Tiger. You know you can't tell a mahmie that's ripe from one that's not. Come on. We've got to get you to the doctor."

He took the tiger into town. While the doctor was working on poor Bra' Tiger's mouth, Bra' Anansi hurried over to the young maiden's house.

"Come," he said. "I want you to see something." He led her to the window of the doctor's office.

There, sure enough, was Bra' Tiger with his mouth open wide, all his front teeth missing!

"Oh, my!" exclaimed the girl.

"You see?" said the spider. "Now will you marry me?"

"Oh, Anansi, Tiger may not have any teeth, but he is so strong! And he can run so fast! Why, he can outrun any horse in the village!"

"Humph!" grumbled the spider. "He ought to. Goodness knows I spend all my time training him."

"What do you mean?" asked the girl.

"Well, Bra' Tiger is my horse. Didn't you know that? I ride him everywhere I want to go."

"I don't believe it. Prove it," said the girl.

Bra' Anansi and Bra' Tiger went back to the jungle. Bra' Tiger found a nice, soft spot beneath a tree. He lay down and began to lick his paws. "Go away, Bra' Anansi. I suppose you mean well, but I seem to have nothing but bad luck when I'm with you."

Bra' Anansi put a hurt look on his face. He left sulkily.

The next morning the tiger awoke hearing a low moaning. He cracked open one eye and twitched his long whiskers. There, hobbling along on the ground, limping badly, was Bra' Anansi.

"I feel ridiculous," he said.

"What's wrong with you, Bra' Anansi? Why are you limping?"

"A lizard almost got me. I think all of my legs are broken. I am trying to get to town to see the doctor. But I may die before I get there."

Bra' Tiger hopped to his feet. "I'll take you," he said. "Climb up on my back."

"That's very kind of you, Bra' Tiger. But I'm so weak I would probably fall off. If we had a saddle and some stirrups, that might help."

Bra' Tiger grumbled that it was silly, but allowed the spider to strap a saddle to his back.

"This is fine. But what am I going to hang onto? We must get you a bit and bridle and reins as well. And I'll need some spurs."

Bra' Tiger complained loudly, but in the end allowed the spider to outfit him.

"I feel ridiculous," he said. "And I look like a horse."

The cat set off, loping gently through the forest. At last they reached the town. To Bra' Tiger's horror, the girl of his dreams was sitting on her front porch! Bra' Tiger turned to go back into the forest. But Bra' Anansi dug his sharp spurs into the tiger's sides. The cat leaped into the air and bolted like lightening! Straight up the steps of the porch he ran, in through the front door and out through the back. He was so embarrassed that he did not stop running until he was deep in the jungle. He did not notice that while running through the house, he had knocked Bra' Anansi out of the saddle. The spider sailed through the air. When he hit the floor he landed smack on a pin. The spider howled in pain. But luckily for him the pin bent when he hit it and he bounced off.

Bra' Tiger hid in the jungle. Never again did he dare to go into town. From that day forward all tigers have been animals of the bush.

And what about Bra' Anansi? Well, he found life in the house much more pleasant. So he stayed on. That is why today spiders still live in houses.

"And if the pin didn't bend, the story wouldn't end."

HAPPY ENDINGS?

Writing through Creative Thinking

In the story, we do not learn whether either Bra' Anansi or Bra' Tiger gets to marry the girl. What do you think happened?

Write the next chapter of the story. Use your own paper if needed.

BENDING THE PIN

Working with the Moral of the Story

When any Bra' Anansi story is told in Belize, it ends with the words, "And if the pin didn't bend, the story wouldn't end." Landing on a pin is Bra' Anansi's punishment for all the terrible things he does to poor Bra' Tiger. But the pin must bend. If it killed Bra' Anansi, there could be no more Bra' Anansi stories. Can you think up another saying to end the story? Remember, Bra' Anansi must not get killed.

Bra' Anansi stories also give us reasons for why things are the way they are in the world. What are two explanations given in this story about where animals live?

We are taught from the time we are very young to be afraid of spiders. But spiders are very useful to man. That is why Bra' Anansi is allowed to remain in the house.

Find out and write about the following:

1. How do spiders help man?

2. How many spiders are poisonous to man?

3. What would happen if we killed all spiders?

Discuss each question with your classmates.

- What does the story teach us about friendship?

- Look up the word *gullible*. Who in the story is gullible?

- Write your own Bra' Anansi story. Write an ending with an explanation about why something is the way it is.

THE FUNNIES

Writing Dialogue

Find a local or national newspaper. Look for the cartoon strip "Calvin and Hobbes." Follow the cartoon strip for several days. Get comic books or watch the cartoons for Sylvester and Tweety Bird, Tom and Jerry, Roadrunner and Coyote, and Bugs Bunny and Elmer Fudd, or Bugs Bunny and Yosemite Sam. Do you see any similarities among those characters and Bra' Anansi and Bra' Tiger?

Make your own cartoon strip for Bra' Anansi and Bra' Tiger. Make the illustrations and write the dialogue for each character. If you wish, make up your own original cartoon strip for two characters where the little, weaker character is always getting the better of the bigger, stronger character.

STRAIGHT FROM THE HORSE'S MOUTH

Object-Specific Vocabulary

In the story, Bra' Anansi fits Bra' Tiger with a saddle, a bridle, stirrups, a bit, and reins. He also uses spurs. Fit the horse below with that gear. Label each piece.

WHERE IN THE WORLD?

Country of Origin

The story of Bra' Anansi and Tiger comes from Belize, in Central America. Find Belize and label it. Label the other countries of Central America.

Answer each question about Belize. You will need to use an encyclopedia.

1. How big is Belize in square miles? In square kilometers?

2. What did it used to be called?

3. When did it gain its independence?

4. What are the geographic features (desert, mountains, plains)?

5. What does the name "Belize" mean? From what people did the word come?

6. What languages are spoken in Belize?

7. What is Belizian Creole?

THE WHITE CAT

n aging king had three sons. Each was bright, strong, and handsome. Any one of the three would have made a good king. Their father the king, however, was not eager to give up his crown.

"What am I to do?" he thought to himself. "The people of my kingdom look at me as if I were an old fool. Even my eldest son hints that I should step down. But I have not yet lost my senses. I still rule well. What am I to do?"

He thought and at last hit upon a plan. He called his sons to him.

"It is the custom," he began, "for the eldest to rule when the father steps down from the throne. But I have three sons and love each one equally. I have watched you grow. Each one of you would make a great king. I shall break with custom. Age will not decide who will be king. Instead, I shall hold a competition. It will not be difficult. But it will help me make my decision. When I retire, I shall want a companion—a loyal, faithful friend. I have decided that whoever brings me the sweetest dog at the end of one year will be king."

The three princes were quite surprised. The eldest was angry. All his life he had thought he would one day be king. The younger two were puzzled but thought their own chances for the throne now looked a little better.

The very next day the three set out. By and by they came to a fork in the road. The road to the right they knew led to a great city. The road to the left led into a thick, dark forest. This forest was said to be haunted. No one would go into it.

"I suggest we take the road to the right," said Henri, the eldest. "It will soon be sundown."

"I agree," said Pierre, the middle son.

"Hmmm," murmured Phillipe, the youngest, "I don't know. I've often wanted to see what lies on the other side of this forest. I think I shall take the road to the left."

"As you wish," replied the older two. "But we shall strike off together. We all shall meet at this spot in one year."

They all agreed, and Phillipe set off alone.

A good path led through the forest, and Phillipe enjoyed the smell of the trees, the babble of the nearby stream, and the songs of the birds. But presently the air grew heavy and the sky became dark. Thunder clapped, and lightning flashed. The prince knew a storm was near.

It rained cats and dogs, as they say. It rained so hard that the prince could not make out the path and strayed from it. In a short time he knew he was lost. He let go of the reins of his horse and let it lead the way.

The prince was soaked to the skin. He was discouraged and was sure his horse was leading him in circles. Then, when he least expected it, he spied a light in the distance. He turned his horse in the direction of the light.

When at last he reached the light, he found himself in front of an enormous castle. "This may be the castle of an ogre," thought the prince, "but I must take my chances. I must get shelter from this storm."

A moat (with great crocodiles in it) surrounded the castle. On the prince's side of the moat was a tall wooden post. Hanging from the post was a great iron bell with a heavy rope attached.

The prince pulled the rope. The bell pealed. A great drawbridge came down over the moat and the castle gate swung open. The prince rode his horse across the drawbridge into a courtyard. To his surprise, he was greeted not by a sentry, but by a small cat.

Phillipe dismounted. Several more cats scurried forward. They led the horse away to the stables. The first cat led the prince into the castle.

He found himself in a cozy room, richly furnished. There were chairs of fine silk fabric. Curtains were of thick, soft velvet. Tapestries—beautiful woven cloths—all with pictures of cats, hung on the walls.

A cheery fire crackled in the fireplace. The cat that had first greeted the prince led him to a chair. Laid out across it was a suit of clothes.

"My size, no doubt," thought the prince, wondering about the strange events of the night.

He was right. The clothes were a perfect fit. They seemed to have been made for him.

He took off his wet garments and put on the dry ones. Then he dozed by the fire. After awhile, he felt a soft pawing at his leg. He awoke and looked down. There at his feet was a beautiful white cat. She jumped up onto the arm of the chair and touched his cheek with her pink nose.

"Are you rested?" she asked.

"Indeed, Miss, I have been well taken care of."

"Come then, you must be hungry."

She led him into a large banquet hall. In its center was a long table. forty people could have sat there comfortably, but only two places were set. One place was at the head of the table, and the other was to the left. She motioned for the prince to take the seat on the left; she seated herself at the head.

What a meal was served! Delicately seasoned dishes for the prince; a mouse, a cricket, and a grasshopper for the cat.

Throughout dinner, Phillipe found the White Cat (for that is what he came to call her) to be most charming. She had a sweet voice, ate with perfect manners, and could discuss any subject with ease. But at dinner's end, she did a strange thing. She opened up a locket that she wore around her neck. She gazed for awhile at a picture within, sighed, and then told the prince good-night. She jumped down from her chair and left the dining hall; the prince was led to his own chambers.

In the morning he heard a commotion, a great noise beneath his bedroom window. Looking out, he saw the White Cat mounted on a greyhound, a very sleek, fast dog. Many other cats were riding dogs of all sizes. Some of the cats were blowing hunting horns.

"Come join us," called the White Cat. "Your horse has already been saddled and is waiting."

The prince found a suit of riding clothes laid out at the foot of his bed. These he put on and hurried downstairs.

What a hunt it was! The White Cat caught a pheasant, two rats and a gopher, several crickets and a grasshopper. The prince was very impressed with her skill! Then the party returned to the palace.

Dinner was just a pleasant as it had been the night before. But at the end of the evening the White Cat opened the locket around her neck, looked at whatever was inside, sighed a sad little sigh, and then bid the prince goodnight.

Every day the White Cat had something new and exciting for the prince to do. He did not even notice that time was flying by. He did not even remember the stormy night in the forest or the quest that had taken him into the forest. He had all but forgotten his brothers, his father, and his father's kingdom.

One night, at dinner, the prince found that the White Cat was very quiet. She barely spoke throughout the meal. Finally he asked her what was wrong.

"Do you know what day it is today, my Prince?"

She simply looked at a portrait inside her locket sighed deeply, and left the room.

"Well, it's Wednesday, I think. No, it's Thursday. Or maybe Saturday... Well, I don't know what day it is, and that's a fact!"

"It's one day short of one year that you have come to me. Tomorrow you must leave. Are you ready to go back?"

The prince leaped from his chair. "Oh, no!" he cried. "How could this have happened? You have bewitched me! I am ruined!"

The White Cat looked at him sadly. A small glass bell lay on the table. The cat rang it, and another cat appeared, carrying a small satin pillow. On the pillow was a walnut. "Take it," the White Cat said. "Inside is what your father has requested."

"Oh, and now you would make fun of me! I thought you cared more for me than that!"

"Take the walnut," repeated the cat. "Hold it up to your ear."

The prince took the walnut from the pillow. He held it up to his ear. Coming from inside he heard the faint bark of a dog.

"Oh, my lovely kitty," said the prince. "How could I have doubted you? How can I ever thank you?"

The White Cat said nothing. She simply looked at a portrait inside her locket—a portrait the prince had never seen—sighed deeply, and left the room.

Morning came. Phillipe heard the clatter of a horse's hooves on cobblestones. He looked out the window. His horse was saddled and ready, sleek and well combed. The prince dressed, put the walnut in his breast pocket, and went down to the courtyard. There was not a cat anywhere to be found. The prince mounted his horse and set off. By sundown he had reached the same fork in the road where he had left his brothers one year before.

They were there waiting for him. Each one had a lovely dog.

"We had just about given up on you," they said. "We have been here all day. You don't have a dog?"

"Well, I saw many," replied Phillipe. "But I could not make up my mind. But I do have a gift."

"What is it?" they asked.

"Oh, just a little something I picked up. We must hurry. The sun is setting."

The older two brothers had secret thoughts of joy. Their younger brother had failed. Perhaps their father would divide the kingdom between the two of them.

End of Part I

IT'S A DOG'S LIFE

Building Topic-Specific Vocabulary through Research

Match each breed of dog given below with its country or continent of origin. Look in an encyclopedia. You may be surprised. An Afghan hound does not come from Afghanistan! Some countries may be used more than once.

1. Poodle
2. Afghan Hound
3. Keeshond
4. Greyhound
5. Whippet
6. Samoyed
7. Lhasa Apso
8. Basset Hound
9. Cocker Spaniel
10. Puli
11. Chihuahua
12. Saint Bernard
13. Akita
14. Boxer
15. Basenji

a. England
b. France
c. Germany
d. Holland
e. Hungary
f. Italy
g. Egypt
h. Nigeria
i. Rhodesia
j. Central Africa
k. Asia
l. Siberia
m. Tibet
n. Mexico
o. Japan

IT'S A DOG'S LIFE

Expanding Topic-Related Vocabulary

Write a description for three breeds of dogs on the previous page. Use the example below as a model. Then make an illustration of the dog beside your description.

1. Poodle
   There are three sizes of this breed. They are the toy, which is the smallest, the miniature, and the standard. All have a thick coat. The coat is wooly underneath and wiry on top. Usually the coat of poodles is clipped. If their hair is allowed to grow, it grows into rope like cords. Poodles may be black, white, brown, gray, cream-colored, or apricot. But their coat should be one solid color. It should not have several colors. Poodles became very popular in France.

IT'S ALL THE SAME TO ME

Working with Synonyms and Antonyms

A synonym is a word that has the same or nearly the same meaning as another word. Example: *bright — smart*

An antonym is a word that has the opposite or nearly the opposite meaning as another word. Example: *bright — stupid*

For each word from the story, write as many synonyms and antonyms as you can on your own paper. Make it a contest. Work in teams.

- strong
- beg
- handsome
- king
- old
- love
- difficult
- loyal
- sweet
- good
- heavy
- dark
- hard
- enormous
- wet
- doze
- sad
- sundown
- rough
- shout
- weep

IT'S RAINING CATS & DOGS

Working with Idiomatic Expressions

Some of our expressions do not mean what the words would suggest. These are called *idioms*.

The story says, "It was raining cats and dogs." This does not mean that cats and dogs were falling out of the clouds. It means that it was raining very hard.

Each sentence contains an idiom. It is underlined. Use the sentence context and what you know about the story to learn the real meaning of each idiom. Circle the best answer.

1. The king had three sons who were bright, handsome, and strong. There were everything a father could hope for. They were the <u>apple of his eye</u>. This means:
   a. They brought him beautiful apples.
   b. He was very proud of them.
   c. Every time he saw them he thought about apples.
   d. Apples were his favorite fruit.

2. Phillipe was lost in the forest. It was raining hard and was very dark. He did not know how he would get out of the forest, but <u>he did not lose heart.</u> This means:
   a. He did not have a heart attack.
   b. His heart was beating fast.
   c. He did not give up hope.
   d. He was not really lost.

3. When he made it through the storm, the prince felt like <u>a cat with nine lives.</u> This means:
   a. He thought he had been turned into a cat.
   b. He felt lucky.
   c. He had the hard life of a cat.
   d. He felt rested and safe.

CHIT CHAT

Doing Research

People can use words or gestures to talk to each other. Do animals talk? If so, how? If not, why not? What is your opinion? What can you find out in an encyclopedia about animal communication? Write or discuss your findings.

Animals certainly do have their own characteristic voice. Match each animal with the sound it makes.

Donkeys	_____	meow
Cats	_____	bleat
Dogs	_____	squawk
Geese	_____	croak
Ducks	_____	bark
Birds	_____	bray
Frogs	_____	moo
Cows	_____	quack
Sheep and goats	_____	oink
Crickets	_____	whinny
Parrots	_____	gobble
Elephants	_____	honk
Seals	_____	chirp
Horses	_____	roar
Pigs	_____	trumpt
Turkeys	_____	buzz
Snakes	_____	chatter
Lions	_____	hiss
Bees	_____	whine
Mice	_____	squeak
Monkeys	_____	
Spoiled children	_____	

Can you name any animals that do not have a voice?

_____ _____ _____

28

Find out about Washoe the chimpanzee and Koko the gorilla. They may not be in the encyclopedia, so ask the librarian to help you. What is so special about them? Write what you find out.

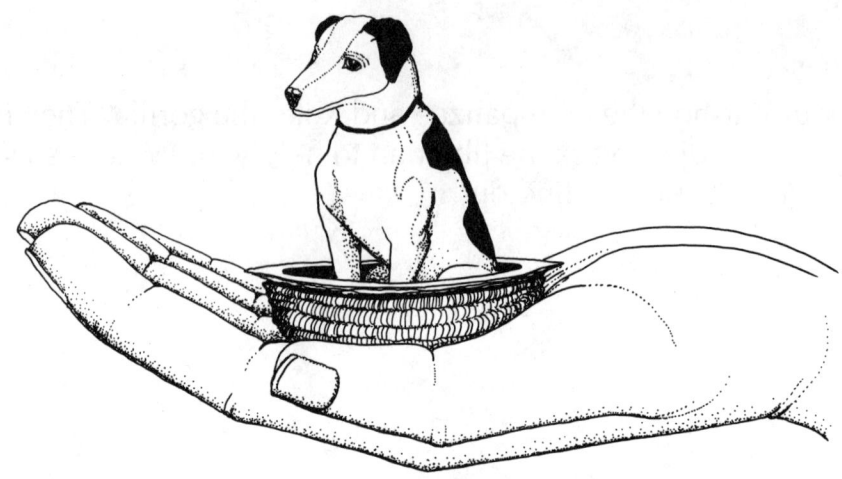

THE WHITE CAT, PART II

y nightfall, the three brothers reached the palace. Their father set off fireworks to welcome them home. Hundreds of townspeople had gathered to see who would win the crown. The courtyard was ablaze with lanterns. A stage had been built in the center for the three princes to present their gifts.

The eldest came forward first. He had a magnificent poodle. The crowd ooed and aahed.

The second stepped forward. He had a majestic Afghan hound. The crowd aahed and ooed.

"And what about you, my son," said the king to his youngest son. "Have you no pet to offer your father?"

"Well, sire, I had a hard time choosing. So I brought you this."

He held out the walnut. The crowd broke into a roar of laughter.

But then he opened the walnut, and the tiniest little dog that ever lived jumped out onto the palm of his hand.

A hush fell over the crowd. The king paled. Henri and Pierre were speechless.

The king looked at each of the dogs carefully. At last he spoke. "These animals are without equal. I could not choose just one to be my companion. I must have all three. So there is a tie. There is not yet a winner in this contest. So I will have another competition. Whichever one of you can bring me, at the end of one year, a fabric so fine that it will fit through the eye of a needle, he will become king."

The older two breathed a sigh of relief. Phillipe smiled. He knew he had won the contest. But he knew his father was not yet ready to give up the throne.

After three days' rest, the three set off again. They took the same paths as the year before.

This time, no storm muddled Phillipe's way. He spurred his horse through the forest and came at last to the castle of the White Cat.

Inside, he found her asleep on a chair and stroked her gently. She yawned and stretched. "Ah, king's son, you have returned to me," she said.

She climbed into his lap and purred softly.

A year went by faster than the tale can tell. The prince was happy—happier than he had ever been. He had all but forgotten what he had set out to do. But the White Cat reminded him, just as she had the year before. This time she gave him not a walnut but a kernel of wheat.

"Do not lose this," she warned. "In it is your claim to the throne. Your father cannot fail to declare you the winner."

The White Cat placed the seed in a small silver box. She handed it to the prince, and he put it in his breast pocket. At dusk he reached the fork in the road. His brothers were waiting.

"Were you successful?" they asked nervously.

"Well you know, a piece of fabric that will fit through the eye of a needle is a hard thing to find. But I have a piece of silk that I think will please Father just as much."

All brothers smiled, each one sure of his own victory.

The palace courtyard was brightly lit. The three young men stepped onto the stage. Henri and Pierre each brought out his own fabric while all eyes watched.

First one needle was tried, then another, and yet another. At last a needle with an eye big enough was found, and the cloth slipped through. The onlookers oohed.

"And what about you, Phillipe. You were not successful?" asked the king.

"Well, I have something here," answered the youth. He seemed to be fumbling around in his pocket. At last he brought out the tiny box, opened it, and took out the wheat.

The king adjusted his spectacles. "What, you mean to help me start a garden? Shall I become a baker when I retire?"

The crowd roared with laughter. The prince did not reply. He cracked open the kernel of wheat and out fell what seemed to be a hair. It did indeed slip through the eye of the tiniest needle of the royal tailor. And when that hair-like thread was unraveled, the most magnificent cloth appeared! Its

And when that hair-like thread was unraveled, the most magnificent cloth appeared!

colors were bright and true, and woven among the threads were scenes of cats.

The crowd was silent. They looked at their king to see what he would do. The older brothers held their breath. They wondered what their father would do.

"Harrumph!" The king's grunt finally broke the silence. "Well, I see I shall have to declare yet another tie! All of these beautiful fabrics passed the test! All three went through the eye of a needle! So I shall hold one final contest. This time there must be a winner. This is how I shall judge. You must each find a princess to be your bride. The son who brings back the princess with the greatest dowry, the greatest marriage gift, he will become king.

Henri and Pierre grumbled. They thought their father was wasting time. They wanted him to decide. But they could say nothing. Phillipe only smiled. He was glad to have one more chance to be with his beloved White Cat.

When the three parted company several days later, he made his way straight to her castle. This time the White Cat herself was at the castle gate to receive him.

"Your father was not pleased with your gift?" she asked.

"My father does not want to stop being king," he replied. "But never mind that. We are together again, and that is all that matters. Who would have thought that one little kitty could have so captured my heart?"

The year fairly flew by. Whether strolling through the White Cat's gardens, watching her chase butterflies, or sitting quietly by the fire with her sleeping on his lap—each moment for Phillipe was a happy one.

But one day the White Cat seemed very sad. "What is wrong, my lovely kitty?" asked the prince.

"Do you love me?" she asked in return.

"Why, of course I do," laughed the prince. "There has never been a sweeter kitty anywhere. And how you do the amazing things you do … well, I'll never know. And never has anyone been kinder to me."

"But do you love me," she repeated, "enough to take me to your kingdom as your own true love?"

The prince frowned. "Oh, my dear," he said, "I see that after all you are just a silly animal." He stroked her chin. "You see, I must take a real princess to my kingdom. I must have a human as a bride. I cannot marry a cat."

"Ah, I see," she said. "Well, then do you love me enough to do one thing for me before I return you to your father?"

"Anything," replied the prince. "Name it, and it will be done."

"Come with me," said the cat.

She led him down a corridor to a locked door. She opened the door and the two went inside a small room. The prince had never been in this room before. It was not like any other in the palace. Its walls were rough, unfinished stones. There were no soft chairs, no bright tapestries. There was only a sword that hung on one wall.

"Take that sword," said the cat, "and take my life."

"What?" shouted the prince. "Never! Never would I do that to my lovely kitty! How could you ask me to do such a thing? Is your heart made of stone like these walls?"

"You promised to do whatever I asked. I cannot be your wife, for I am a cat. But I cannot live without you. You must do it."

The prince wept and begged and pleaded. But the White Cat was firm. At last, with trembling hand the prince took the sword from the wall. One last time he begged her to change her mind, but she would not. He closed his eyes and with one stroke …

When at last he looked up, he could not believe his eyes. There, standing before him, was the most beautiful maiden he had ever seen.

"Who are you?" he asked. "And where is my kitty?"

"I am she," replied the lady. "And I am princess of this castle and many other kingdoms besides. An evil sorcerer had me under a spell. Only a great love, only a man who trusted me completely could break that spell. Look at the portrait in this locket."

The prince was amazed to see his own picture.

"And now," said the princess, "will you take me to your kingdom as your bride?"

The king could no longer question his youngest son's right to the throne. But the White Cat refused it.

"I give as a gift a kingdom to each of your sons. And you sire, may be old, but you have not stopped being a good king. Rule your own kingdom until the end of your days."

And the king did exactly that.

VIVE LA FRANCE!

Country of Origin

The story "The White Cat" comes from France. Below is a map of France and the countries that border it. Label the countries. Locate the capital of France. The youngest prince had his adventures in a big forest. Locate a big forest in France and draw it on your map. What is its name? (Hint: It is near Paris.)

Answer each question. Add the new information to your map.

1. What sea is to the north of France?

2. What sea is to the south of France?

3. What ocean touches France?

4. What is the smallest country that borders France? How big is it in square miles? What is the largest country?

MY KINGDOM FOR A HORSE

History

These kings were kings of France. Match each king with his period of reign (when he ruled). Write one fact about each king. You will need to use an encyclopedia. Begin thinking about what the Roman numerals mean after each king's name.

King Charles II the Bald	_____	1180-1223
King Charles III the Simple	_____	1285-1314
King Charles III the Fat	_____	1589-1610
King Charles IV	_____	843-877
King Charles V	_____	1643-1715
King Philip II Augustus	_____	893-922
King Philip III	_____	1328-1350
King Philip IV the Fair	_____	882-887
King Philip VI of Valois	_____	1610-1643
King Louis VIII the Lionhearted	_____	1223-1226
King Louis IX	_____	1270-1285
King Louis XIII	_____	1322-1328
King Louis XIV The Sun King	_____	1226-1270

WHEN IN ROME DO AS THE ROMANS DO

Math

In the exercise on the previous page, you saw that each king had letters beside his name. The Romans of long ago used these letters as numbers. They are called *Roman numerals*.

Look at these numbers.

I	II	III	IV	V	VI	VII	VIII	IX	X
1	2	3	4	5	6	7	8	9	10

XI	XII	XIII	XIV	XV	XVI	XVII	XVIII	XIX	XX
11	12	13	14	15	16	17	18	19	20

XXX	XL	L	LX	LXX	LXXX	XC	C	CX	CL
30	40	50	60	70	80	90	100	110	150

CD	CDL	D	DL	CM	M	ML	MC	MD	MM
400	450	500	550	900	1000	1050	1100	1500	2000

Do you see the pattern?
The important letters are

I	V	X	L	C	D	M
1	5	10	50	100	500	1000

A letter before one of equal or greater value subtracts from the value:
XXIX = 29
A letter after one of equal or greater value adds to the value: DC = 600.

Write each Roman numeral as a number.

LXIV _____   XXXV _____   CI _____   CDXCIX _____
XLII _____   LIII _____   II _____   CCCVII _____

Write each number as Roman numerals.

12 _____   72 _____   89 _____   1019 _____
825 _____   2300 _____   590 _____   68 _____

Dictate numbers to a partner. Have your partner write each number as a Roman numeral. Switch. Have your partner dictate numbers to you.

For each king on the previous page, change the Roman numeral to a modern number.

NOTHING PHONY ABOUT IT

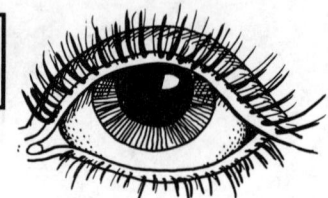

Homophones

Homophones are words that sound the same but are spelled differently and have different meanings.

The first word of each pair appeared in the story. Below it is its homophone. Write a simple definition for each word.

seen _____

scene _____

pale _____

pail _____

one _____

won _____

eye _____

I _____

days _____

daze _____

tale _____

tail _____

kernel _____

colonel _____

piece _____

peace _____

hair _____

hare _____

marry _____

merry _____

I SHALL RETURN!

Shall vs. *Will*

Study this table. It explains the helping verb shall *or* will.

	Singular	**Plural**
1st Person	I shall *or* I will go.	We shall *or* we will go.
2nd Person	You will go.	You (all) will go.
3rd Person	He will go.	They will go.
	She will go.	The men will go.
	It will go.	The women will go.
	The cat will go.	The dogs will go.
	The prince will go.	The people will go.
	The letter will go.	The letters will go.

If something is going to happen in the future, we use the helping verb *shall* or *will* with another verb. But *shall* is used only in the first person, that is, with *I* or *we*. It usually is used to say something strongly, for emphasis: I shall win this contest.

Rewrite each sentence to show future tense. Use shall *or* will + *the underlined verb. The underlined verb will not have an ending on it. The first one is done for you*

1. The king <u>wants</u> only a sweet-tempered dog.

    The king will want only a sweet-tempered dog.

2. Philipe <u>took</u> the road to the left.

3. The White Cat <u>greeted</u> the prince.

4. She <u>gives</u> him everything he needs.

5. "We <u>tried</u> to catch grasshoppers," she said.

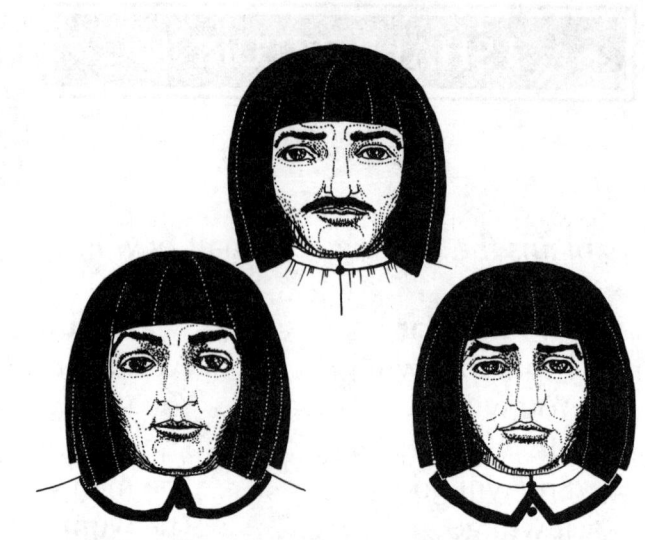

THREE BROTHERS

hree brothers set out to seek their fortune. Their father had died. He had left each son a strong horse, a finely crafted sword, and these words of advice:
"Tell the truth and keep your promises; your word is your bond. Do not be boastful; pride comes before a fall. Do not be lazy; life will reward you."

The young men left their home. They rode for several days. They came at last to the edge of a great forest. Nightfall was near.

Danilo, the eldest, spoke. "We must make camp here. We do not know our way through this forest. Wild beasts and highwaymen make their home in these woods. Animals we might overcome, but robbers would surely kill us if we stumbled upon their camp. We shall wait until daylight. I shall take the first watch. Gavrilo, you take the second, and Ivan you will take the third."

They all agreed. Danilo began his watch while his brothers slept. After awhile, he heard a noise coming from the trees. Sensing danger, he entered the forest. Sure enough, there lay a lion, crouching, waiting for the chance to seize its sleeping prey. Danilo caught the lion off guard. The great cat sprang at Danilo. Danilo raised his sword. The lion landed on the lifted sword and was pierced through the heart. Danilo cut a strip from the lion's hide, tied it around his waist, and returned to the camp. He did not even awaken his brothers. Gavrilo and Ivan took their turns watching. Nothing else special happened, and the three left at daybreak.

They entered the forest and made slow progress throughout the day. By nightfall they had reached the shores of a great lake and decided to make camp there.

Gavrilo, the middle brother, spoke. "Tonight I will take the first watch. Ivan, you and Danilo can follow me."

Again they agreed. While his brothers slept, Gavrilo kept watch. The moon rose and flung a crinkled silver net over the still waters of the lake. Gavrilo saw something move below the surface of the water. It was huge. It was silent, but not so silent as to not make waves that washed upon the shore with a lap, lap, lap. Whatever it was reached the shore and crawled out. It was a great snake, greater and bigger around than any that Gavrilo had ever heard about or seen. Noiselessly, it slithered toward the sleeping men. It meant to crush them with its great body and swallow them whole.

Gavrilo stood ready. He made not a sound. The forked tongue of the great snake flicked in and out, searching out danger, but it did not notice Gavrilo. Gavrilo crashed his sword down upon the skull of the snake. It recoiled violently once, and then fell limp. Gavrilo cut a strip from its back. He tied it around his waist, pushed the dead snake into the water, watched as it sank, then returned to his post. Nothing further happened. Nothing of importance happened during the turns at watch that Ivan and Danilo took, either.

On the following day the three went deeper into the forest. They reached a rough clearing and decided to make camp for the night. Ivan would watch first. While his brothers slept, he moved away from the camp site to gather wood for the fire. As he poked about for dry timber, he suddenly felt the point of sharp steel in his back. He raised up slowly, arms in the air to show surrender.

A hooded man motioned him forward. Ivan knew he had stumbled onto the camp of a band of highwaymen.

Once in the camp, Ivan greeted the robbers boldly.

"Captain," he said to the chieftain, "I have travelled for many days in search of your band. I need teachers to master your trade. Alone, I have learned much. I can enter any locked building as quietly as a cat. I can sniff out gold and silver. But I have taught myself all I can. Take me in as your student."

"Are you any good at spying?" asked the captain.

"Yes, and climbing and entering unheard," replied Ivan.

"Good. You will come with us tonight on a job we have to do. If you prove yourself worthy, you will stay with us. If you do not, we will kill you."

Ivan had no choice but to agree.

That night, the band of robbers made their way to the tzar's palace. They told Ivan to climb the wall and find the positions of the guards. This he did.

Gavrilo stood ready. He made not a sound.

Finding all the guards fast asleep, he returned to the wall and whispered to the waiting highwaymen.

"Psst. The guards are asleep. Climb the wall quickly and jump down. I will help you, and I will keep watch from this side."

The men climbed the wall one by one. But when they jumped down they jumped onto the waiting dagger of the pretending apprentice. One by one Ivan slew them all.

Ivan entered the palace. He found himself in the bed chamber of one of the princesses. It was the tzar's youngest daughter. She was lovelier than a rose, and Ivan could not take his eyes from her. She wore a gold ring on her finger as she slept. Ivan carefully pulled it off and slipped it onto his little finger.

He entered the next room. The tzar's second daughter lay sleeping. She, too, was a great beauty. Ivan removed a golden bracelet that she wore on her arm and slipped it into his pocket.

He entered a third room and found a third maiden sleeping. She was the tzar's eldest daughter, and even in her sleep her beauty was dazzling. He took a golden necklace from around her neck and put it into his pocket. Then he left the palace. He leaped as noiselessly as a cat over the wall and returned to his sleeping brothers.

In the morning the three rode out of a forest and before long came to the town. The tzar's criers were everywhere!

"Hear ye, hear ye!" they called. "Last night twelve dangerous robbers were slain in the palace garden. The night before, the King of All Snakes was slain. The night before, the King of All Cats was slain. Anyone able to solve these wondrous mysteries shall be richly rewarded."

The three brothers looked at one another. Each one had his own secret.

"Let us speak together of the last three nights," said Danilo.

Each shared his adventure. Afterwards, they shook hands and set off for the palace.

The tzar called the three brothers forward. "Do you know anything about the events of the last three days?" he asked.

"We do," answered the three.

"What do you know?" asked the tzar.

"I killed the lion," said Danilo simply. He lifted his tunic to reveal the hide belt.

"I slew the great snake," said Gavrilo. He showed the ribbon of snakeskin around his waist.

"I slew the highwaymen," said Ivan, "and took as a reward a piece of jewelry from each of your daughters."

The tzar was dumbstruck. When at last he spoke, he said: "Braver, more fearless men I have never known. I would have you as my sons-in-law. Will you marry my daughters?"

The eldest brother spoke. "Sire," he said, "we know not the ways of tzars. Our father was a simple farmer. He taught us to work hard and be honest. That is all we know."

"I may be a tzar. But I am also a father. I wish for my daughters husbands of noble character more than husbands of noble birth."

The three brothers were impressed with the tzar's words. They married the three maidens and came to live in the tzar's palace. The tzar was fond of each of his sons-in-law but grew to love the youngest, Ivan, like a true son.

One day the tzar was napping in his garden. A poisonous snake crawled out from behind a bush and poised to strike the king. Ivan happened to be near. He drew his sword and sliced it in two and threw the two halves into the bush. At this moment the tzar awoke. He saw Ivan standing sword in hand. Not knowing what had happened and not asking, he imagined the worst.

"This young man is not who I thought he was," he thought. "He means to betray me, to kill me and become ruler of this land."

He went to his prime minister and told him his fears.

Now, this prime minister had a son of his own, just about Ivan's age. He had hoped his own son would some day marry one of the princesses. When Ivan and his brothers appeared out of nowhere and won the hearts of the entire town, the prime minister became very jealous. "Here is my chance," he thought, "to get rid of this little wretch once and for all!"

"Your Majesty," whimpered the prime minister, "I did try to warn you, you know. I told you that you knew nothing of these men, of their backgrounds. And you mustn't forget that Ivan stole jewelry from the princesses! He's a sly one, he is! Saying he took it as reward. I'd watch him, if I were you. But don't let me worry you."

Well, of course the tzar became *very* worried. So worried, in fact, that he ordered Ivan to be put in prison.

The youngest princess, Ivan's wife, was overcome with grief. She cried and tore at her hair. She would not eat or drink or leave her bed. At last her father had to give in. He commanded Ivan to be brought to him.

"Traitor!" he cried. "You would kill a man who loved you like a son!"

"Father-in-law," began Ivan, "listen to this story."

And he told him the story of the parrot.

End of Part I

STRANGER THINGS HAVE HAPPENED

Developing Divergent Thinking Skills

Each question below is a little bit odd. They all use an adjective that you would probably never use to describe pairs of nouns. In each sentence, the adjective is underlined once. The nouns are in italics.

Think about each question. Write an answer. There are no right answers. Just use your imagination.

1. Which is hungrier, a *forest* or a *lake*? Why?

   _____

   _____

2. Which is prouder, a *sword* or a *gun*? Why?

   _____

   _____

3. Which are redder, *princes* or *highwaymen*? Why?

   _____

   _____

4. Which is braver, a *palace* or a *wall*? Why?

   _____

   _____

5. Which is angrier, a *skull* or a *heart*? Why?

   _____

   _____

A ROSE IS A ROSE IS A ROSE

Homonyms

In the story "The White Cat" we learned about homophones. *Homonyms* are words that are spelled the same and sound the same but have different meanings.

These words appear in the story "Three Brothers." Each word has more than one meaning. Write two sentences for each word using the different meanings.

bond _____

_____

fall _____

_____

watch _____

_____

strip _____

_____

can _____

_____

hide _____

_____

rose _____

_____

band _____

_____

A ROSE BY ANY OTHER NAME

Working with Synonyms

There are many words that mean the same or about the same. These are called *synonyms*.

Replace each underlined word in the sentence with a synonym from the box. Rewrite the sentence.

border	ferocious	robbers	leaped	came	down
told	look for	courageously	scale	castle	money
huge	animals	burglars	killed	lifted	places
watchmen	stabbed	wicked	called to	cat	woods

1. Three brothers set out to <u>seek</u> their <u>fortunes</u>.

2. They came at last to the <u>edge</u> of a <u>great</u> <u>forest</u>.

3. <u>Wild</u> <u>beasts</u> and <u>highwaymen</u> make their home in this forest.

4. The <u>lion</u> <u>sprang</u> at Danilo.

5. The lion <u>landed</u> on the <u>upraised</u> sword and was <u>pierced</u> through the heart.

6. Ivan <u>greeted</u> the robbers <u>boldly</u>.

7. They <u>instructed</u> Ivan to <u>climb</u> the wall and find the <u>positions</u> of the guards.

THE KING OF BEASTS

Science

Scientists divide living things into categories called *kingdoms.* The two most well-known kingdoms are the *plant kingdom* and the *animal kingdom.*

In the animal kingdom are many different kinds of animals. Some have a shell, some have only a soft body (like jellyfish), some have six legs, some have eight, some have a backbone, and some do not.

For each class of animals, write the name of the biggest living animal within that class. Here are some ideas about how you can find out the information:

1. Start by talking to the reference librarian of your school or local library.
2. Talk to a teacher in your school's science department.
3. Call the science department of a nearby college or university.
4. Call a natural history museum. Experts in these areas are very happy to help us with our research projects!

INSECTS

SPIDERS

FISH

AMPHIBIANS

REPTILES

BIRDS

SLIPPERY WHEN WET

Science

In "Three Brothers" there is a great snake. Find out some information about snakes.

1. In the animal kingdom, to what class do snakes belong?

   _____

2. How many different types of snakes are there in the world?

   _____

3. Name and illustrate five poisonous snakes. Where do they come from?

   _____

4. How do snakes move?

   _____

5. Are they warm-blooded or cold-blooded? What does that mean?

   _____

6. How do they have offspring? Do they lay eggs?

   _____

7. Why do they shed their skin?

   _____

8. How do they shed their skin?

   _____

9. What do they eat?

   _____

THREE BROTHERS, PART II

ere is the story about the parrot: There lived a great and powerful tzar. He was rich and surrounded himself with rare and wonderful things. His favorite possession was a parrot brought to him from a far, faraway land. This parrot could talk and told the tzar all the things he wanted to hear.

The tzar, in turn, gave the parrot everything that he could imagine that a parrot might desire. He gave him a golden cage, seeds, nuts, and berries, a perch, and a swing from which he could hang upside-down.

But the parrot was not happy.

One day the tzar asked him why.

The parrot replied, "You have your family and friends around you. You may see them whenever you wish. My family and friends are far away. I miss them. I would like to see them."

"Oh," said the tzar, "how can I let you go? How can I trust that you will come back to me? I am afraid that once you spread your wings upon the wind, you will forget all about me. Then what will I do?"

"Let me go," said the parrot, "just for three weeks. I promise I will come back."

The tzar had learned that if you would be great and powerful, you could trust no one. He did not trust the parrot. But he loved his colorful feathered companion more than anything else in the world. So he agreed. He opened the caged door. The parrot hopped out onto the ledge. He stretched his wings, stiff from months of no use. Then he squawked joyfully, leaped into the air, flapped his wings, and was gone.

The parrot flew for six days without stopping. He flew over mountains and steppes. He flew over forests and deserts. He flew over a great ocean. At last he flew atop a great jungle, green from daily rain and steaming from the hot sun. A great river wound through the trees. He was home! He dipped down into the trees and perched on a branch, singing gaily.

Monkeys chattered. Macaws squawked. Sloths opened a lazy eye. Word spread fast through the jungle that the traveler had returned.

What a family reunion! What playful pecking and preening! What a symphony of sound! Mother and father, brothers and sisters, aunts and uncles and cousins flocked for the homecoming. For three days and three nights the parrot told of all his adventures in foreign lands. He told of the tzar, of the golden cage, of the sweet things he had to eat, of being able to sleep without fearing the coils of a python. Then he played in the tropical forest to his heart's content.

On the fifth day of his visit his sister came to him. "You were born to be free," she said. "You were not meant to live in a cage, no matter how it shines. Stay here with us. Do not return to the tzar."

The parrot thought.

On the sixth day his brother came to him. "The tzar does not love you," he said. "He only wants you as a toy, as a creature to amuse him. He is not of your kind. Leave him. He will never find you here."

The parrot thought.

On the seventh day the parrot called his family to him. "Tomorrow I will return to the tzar. I made a promise to him. I am no less free in my home with you than a fish who must always watch out for alligators. The tzar has proved that he does love me. He let me go. He will let me go again. I know. I will see you again."

And he departed.

Before he left the jungle he went to a secret spot where he knew of a magical fruit. The fruit could heal the sick or make the old grow young. He plucked three of these and carried them back to the tzar's kingdom.

Imagine the tzar's joy when he saw his companion before him. He wept tears of joy. He gently stroked the back of the parrot's neck. "No more will you be locked up in a cage," he said. "You may live in the garden or perch in the trees. At night you may sleep in my room where you will be safe and warm."

The parrot thanked the tzar. He dropped the fruit into his hands and told him of their great power. The tzar was very excited. He told his prime minister to prepare one of the fruits that very minute.

But the prime minister took the monarch aside and whispered in his ear.

He dropped the fruit into his hands and told him of their great power.

"Do you not think it strange that we have never before heard of such a fruit as this? Do you not think it strange that a mere parrot could know what we do not? Test the parrot's gift first. Test it on the geese in the barnyard."

The tzar thought. He remembered how the parrot had wanted his freedom. The prime minister's words seemed like wise advice.

"Do it," he said.

The prime minister took the piece of fruit. But before he took it to the barnyard he filled it with poison. When the geese had eaten just a bite they fell down dead.

"Traitor!" cried the tzar. He seized the parrot by the neck and flung him, and in so doing broke the poor creature's neck.

The parrot was dead. The tzar was miserable. He could not understand his companion's betrayal.

Some time later a criminal was caught and sentenced to be hanged. But the tzar, rembering the fruit, ordered that one be given to the condemned man. What was everyone's surprise when the man became young and handsome and strong before all eyes!

The youngest brother ended the story. "Come with me to the garden," he said.

The two walked to the place where the tzar had been sleeping. Ivan went behind the bush and brought out the halves of the deadly snake.

"Your majesty, my brothers and I will take leave of you. We are grown men with wives. Our father's home can be our home no longer. That was our childhood home. And neither can our wives' father's home be our home. That was their childhood home. We will take our wives and find our own way in this world. Those who are filled with jealousy would have us fall. That is because they themselves are weak. Pity them. Now let us go."

BIRDS OF A FEATHER FLOCK TOGETHER

Building Topic-Specific Vocabulary

Complete the table for some of the many birds of the world. One has been done for you.

	Cuckoos	Emus	Flamingos	Hummingbirds	Ostriches	Parrots	Penguins	Quail	Storks
Eats Seed, Plant, or Insect					yes				
Bird of Prey					no				
Sleeps in the Night					yes				
Sleeps in the Day					no				
Bill					yes				
Beak					no				
Web-Footed					no				
Weight					136 kg				
Height					260 cm				
Length					180 cm				
Swims					no				
Walking or Running Bird					yes				
Flying Bird					no				
Where it Lives					Africa				

BIRDS OF A FEATHER FLOCK TOGETHER, PART II

Learning to Categorize

Use the information from the table on the previous page. Group the birds into categories.

Flightless Birds	Birds of Prey
Water Birds	Seed, Plant, or Insect Eaters

Answer each question on your own paper.

1. In general, what characteristic do all birds who swim share?

2. In general, what kinds of birds have bills?

3. What is the largest bird living?

4. What is the smallest bird living?

5. Which birds has only two toes?

6. Which bird has the largest wing span (the distance between the tips of opened wings)?

7. Why do some birds have sharp beaks and some birds have bills?

BIRDS OF A FEATHER FLOCK TOGETHER, PART III

Presenting Information In Visual Form

Choose four birds from the table for the first exercise. Illustrate them. Be sure to include the name of each bird.

BIRDS OF A FEATHER FLOCK TOGETHER, PART IV

Using a Legend or Key

Use the key to discover the mystery animal.

1 - Red   2 - Green   3 - Blue   4 - Brown
5 - Black   6 - White   7 - Yellow

INTO THE WILD BLUE YONDER

Geography

Birds migrate. They move from one place to another as the seasons and climate change. Some fly hundreds, or even thousands, of miles.

In our story, the parrot flew from the tzar's palace to his homeland. But the story does not tell you where that homeland is. It could be in a number of places, because parrots live in many places in the world.

Use the clues in the story. Decide where the parrot went. Your answer might not be the same as those of your classmates. On the map, draw the flying path of the parrot. Then label all the continents. Draw in and name the river. Label the oceans. Figure out, in miles or kilometers, the distance he traveled.

THE WORLD

WASSILISSA THE BEAUTIFUL

 merchant had everything his heart desired. He had fields of tall, golden wheat; he had stables of swift stallions and mares; he had green pastures with fat, lazy grazing cows and thick-coated sheep. He had a house in the city and a house in the country. He had, in fact, just about everything that money could buy.

The merchant was married to a beautiful and sweet woman. They had one lovely daughter called Wassilissa. As a baby, Wassilissa was as beautiful as the dawn. And as she grew, she became lovelier and sweeter with each passing day. She was so beautiful that the townsfolk could not help but call her "Wassilissa the Beautiful."

The merchant looked around at all he had. He folded his arms and smiled with pride and joy.

But as surely as the seasons change, so did the merchant's luck. When Wassilissa was but eight years old, the merchant's wife became ill. No doctors could cure her. Within a short time she would clearly die.

The woman called her young daughter to her bedside. "My child, I must die. I know you will be sad, but you are not to be sad and gloomy forever. I leave you with my blessing and with a great gift. But the gift is a secret. Tell no one about it. Show it to no one."

She pressed something between Wassilissa's palms. Wassilissa looked and saw a rough, hand-carved wooden doll. It was no more than four or five inches tall and not pretty at all.

"Put it in your apron pocket, Wassilissa, *now*. Keep it with you always. If ever you are in trouble, or feel sad or alone, the doll will help you. Go to a quiet place. Give the doll something to eat and drink. It will listen to your trouble and tell you what to do."

The mother gave her little daughter a kiss and then she died.

Wassilissa wept and wept. Night came. The child could not sleep, and the tears would not stop. Wassilissa remembered her mother's gift. She crept out of her little bed and made her way into the kitchen. All of the servants were fast asleep. The girl looked around and found a piece of bread and a little cider. These she took to her room and lay before the wooden doll. Before long, the eyes of the doll began to shine like coals. Its body quivered like a leaf in the wind. It became alive. It ate a bit of the bread and drank a sip of the cider, then turned to Wassilissa.

"Sweet Wassilissa, dry your tears. Go to bed and have sweet dreams. The morning is wiser than the evening."

Wassilissa went back to bed. Soon she fell fast asleep. When she awoke in the morning her grief was not quite so great.

The merchant mourned the death of his wife for many months. But he became worried that Wassilissa might be needing a mother. He at last met a woman in town who was a widow. She came from an important family of good reputation. But most importantly (for the merchant) she had two daughters of her own who were Wassilissa's age.

"This match will be good for Wassilissa," he thought. She will have a mother's love, and two sweet sisters besides." So he asked the widow to marry him.

Now the woman cared not at all for the merchant or his daughter. But she saw a golden opportunity for herself and her daughters, so she accepted.

They had a splendid wedding, and for a time all went well. But Wassilissa's stepmother favored her own daughters. Unlike Wassilissa, they were homely and had evil tempers. As they grew older, they became as ugly as the way they behaved, and no one wanted to be around them. Wassilissa received many proposals of marriage; they did not.

This made Wassilissa's stepmother very angry. It made her stepsisters jealous. Their hatred became so great that they plotted to kill Wassilissa.

From time to time, the merchant had to go away on business. Wassilissa's stepmother waited until he took a trip that would keep him away for many months. She went to him, complaining.

"I am so tired of the noise and trouble of the city," she said. "Let us stay in your country home while you are gone. It is more peaceful there. The sky is bluer. The air is not filled with smoke. We will be happier."

The merchant had the servants pack up the household. He moved his family to the country and then departed.

This was the home of the Baba Yaga, a terrible witch.

Now, it so happened that the merchant's country home lay at the edge of a great forest. In a clearing in this forest was a strange little house which stood upon hen's legs. This was the home of the Baba Yaga, a terrible witch. Baba Yaga let no one near her house. She ate anyone who approached. With their bones she made a fence that stretched all the way around her yard. On top of the fence were human skulls.

Every day, Wassilissa's stepmother sent her into the forest. She hoped the Baba Yaga would catch her and eat her. But with the help of the little doll, Wassilissa always returned safely.

The stepmother thought of a plan. One night she called the three girls to her. She gave them each a task. One of her daughters she asked to knit; the second she told to crochet. Wassilissa was told to spin. Then the mother went through the house and blew out all the candles except one. She pretended to straighten the wick of this one and put the flame out.

"Oh my, how clumsy of me! I've put out the only light in the house!" she exclaimed. "Now how will you see to do your sewing?"

"The light of the moon shines upon our silver needles, Mother," said one of the girls. "We have light enough to do our work. But Wassilissa can do nothing. Her spinning wheel is made of wood."

"True enough," said the mother. " Wassilissa, you may not sit there like a bump on a log. Since you cannot work you must go and borrow fire for us. I have heard that the Baba Yaga has a fire that never goes out. Go into the forest. Borrow fire from the Baba Yaga. Do not come back without it."

She pushed Wassilissa outside and locked the door behind her.

Wassilissa knew that her stepmother intended to kill her. She was terrified. But she knew she had her doll in her apron pocket. She started off.

The forest was thick and the way was hard. Brambles tore at Wassilissa's clothes. Roots and low vines tripped her and made her fall. But she did not stop.

Suddenly she heard the sound of galloping hoofs behing her. She turned and saw a horseman approaching. He was dressed all in white and rode a milk-white horse. He seemed not even to notice Wassilissa. When he passed it became lighter. Dawn came. A short time later Wassilissa again heard a horse's hoofs. A second rider approached. He was dressed from head to toe in red, and he rode a blood-red horse. When he passed, the sun rose.

Wassilissa walked on. At last she reached the hut in the clearing. Wassilissa stared at the horrible wall with its skull lamps and its gate locked with rows of grinning teeth. She trembled in fear, frozen to the spot. A third horseman approached. He was dressed all in black and rode a coal-black horse. He reached the wall, leaped over it, and disappeared, as if swallowed up by the earth. Night fell. The eyes of the skulls began to glitter with an eerie orange light.

End of Part I

AS LOVELY AS A ROSE

Working with Comparative Adjectives

An adjective is a word that describes a noun (a person, place, or thing): a red ball, a quiet room, a small child.

In the story we learn that Wassilissa is lovely. "Lovely" is an adjective. It tells us how Wassilissa looks. Then the story says that she became *lovelier* with each passing day. This means she became more lovely.

To adjectives ending in y, *change the* y *to* i *and add* er *to make the word mean "more."*

1. Wassilissa's stepsisters had _____ tempers than anyone else in town. (ugly)

2. The merchant was _____ with his first wife. (happy)

3. The merchant's new wife bought _____ clothes than his first wife did (costly)

4. With a bigger family to take care of, the merchant became _____ than ever. (busy)

5. _____ girls were nowhere to be found in town. (Messy)

6. Wassilissa's stepmother and stepsisters became _____ and _____ when only Wassilissa had marriage proposals. (angry)

7. The city was _____ and _____ than the country. (noisy) (smoky)

8. The house was chilly in the winter. But the forest was _____ (chilly)

9. "We must think of a _____ plan," said the stepmother to her daughters. (tricky)

10. Every day that Wassilissa returned from the forest, the women became _____ and _____. (grouchy)

A HORSE OF A DIFFERENT COLOR

Word Associations

In the story, three horsemen ride by Wassilissa. Each one is riding a horse of a different color, and is dressed in the same color as his horse. Wassilissa learns that these horsemen are daybreak, the sun, and night.

There are many things that do not have color. But often colors become associated with these things.

Give a color to each of the following. Explain why you chose the color. Do not work with a partner! Work alone. There are no right or wrong answers.

What color is love? Why?

_____

What color is hatred? Why?

_____

What color is anger? Why?

_____

What color is something that's funny? Why?

_____

What color is something that's sad? Why?

_____

What color is a thought? Why?

_____

What color is hope? Why?

_____

WHAT COLOR IS LOVE?

Creating a Bar Graph

Use the results from the last activity for this exercise. Answer each question.

1. What color did you choose most often when giving colors to color-less things?

_____

2. What color did the class use most often?

_____

3. Discuss some possible reasons why.

_____

4. Divide the class into groups or partners. Each team will make two or three bar graphs to show how the class "colored" each item from the previous page. Your graph may look something like this:

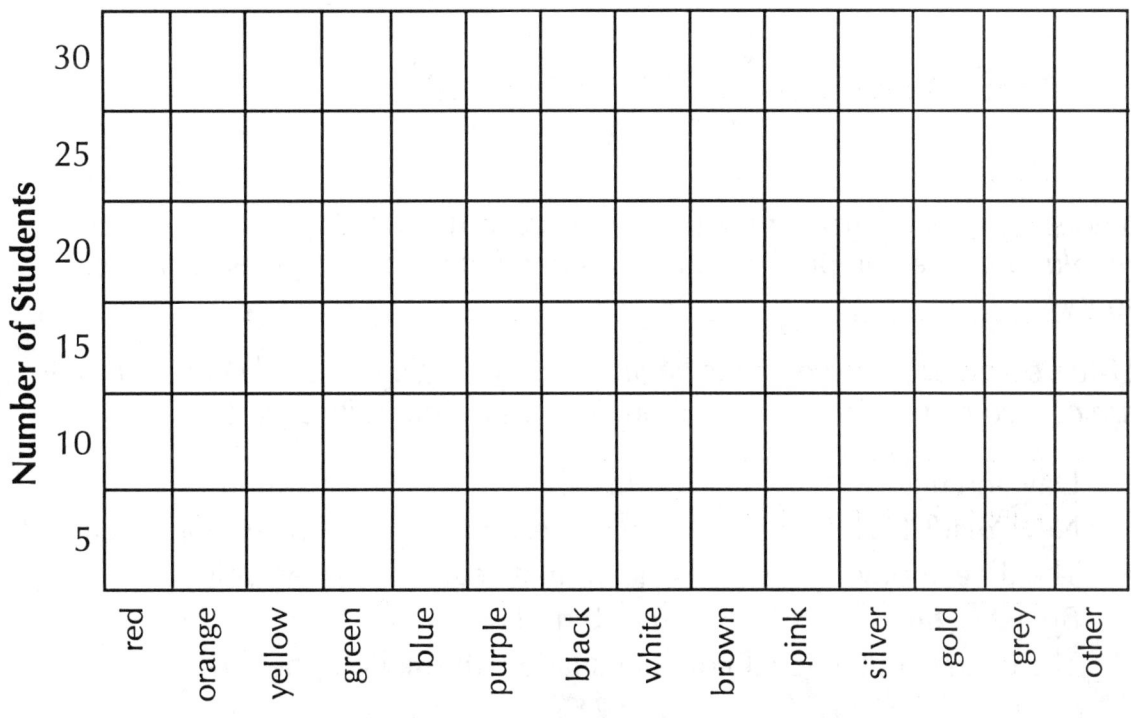

What Color is Love?

AS THE WORLD TURNS

Physical Geography

In the fairy tale, a magical explanation is given for how daybreak, daytime, and nighttime come. What explanation does the story give?
    But we know that the times of day and seasons of the year are caused by how the earth moves. The earth moves in several ways.

Look at each diagram.

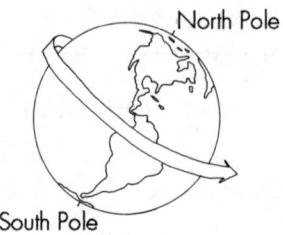

The earth spins around like a top. It spins on its *axis*. It makes one full turn every twenty-four hours. This is called a *rotation*. One rotation is one full day. When where you live faces the sun, it is daytime. When where you live faces away from the sun, it is nighttime.

The earth also moves around the sun, like this:

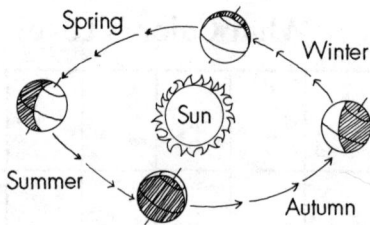

It goes all the way around the sun once every 365 1/4 days. This is called a *revolution*. One complete revolution is one full year. This gives us the seasons.

Listed below are twelve things having to do with time. Decide whether they are caused by rotation *or* revolution. *You may work with a partner.*

Day and night	Winter	Summer
New Year's Day	The longest day	The shortest day
The time of day	The time of year	Midnight
Breakfast time	Your birthday	

The change in the length of your shadow throughout the day

NO BONES ABOUT IT

Science

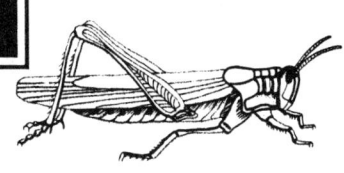

In the story, we read that Baba Yaga's wall is made of bones. Its lamps are skulls.

Bones come from a *skeleton*. Many animals have a bony skeleton, but many do not.

Form small groups of three. For each animal, discuss whether it does or does not have a bony skeleton. Then write the name of that animal in the correct column.

Has a Bony Skeleton	Does Not Have a Bony Skeleton

snake   jellyfish
sponge   giraffe
gorilla   worm
octopus   shark
salmon   tuna
clam   crab
lizard   alligator
oyster   lobster
cow   bumblebee
human   koala bear
pelican   grasshopper
parakeet   whale
seal   tarantula

WASSILISSA, PART II

assilissa heard a whirring sound. She looked around. Flying toward the hut in a huge iron grinding bowl called a mortar was the Baba Yaga. She was driving it with its grinder, or its pestle and sweeping away the tracks behind her with a broom.

She shouted out a command. The sharp grinning teeth that locked the gate snapped apart. The gate swung open. Baba Yaga stepped out of her mortar and sniffed the air.

"I smell a smell that is Russian!" she cried.

Still trembling, the young maiden stepped forward. "It is I, Grandmother, Wassilissa. My stepmother sent me to you to ask for some fire."

"Humph!" grunted the old woman. "Yes, I know her. So she would have my fire, would she? Well, we shall see. I do not give away my fire. You will have to work for it. You will stay with me for three days. You will clean my house and cook my dinner. You will do whatever chores I give you. If you do all I ask, you shall have the fire your stepmother seeks. If you do not, I will eat you."

With that, the old witch strode into the house. Wassilissa followed behind. Baba Yaga climbed upon the hearth by the fireplace. "Bring me my dinner," she ordered. "I am hungry."

Wassilissa set food and drink upon the table. There was enough for ten strong men, but the witch gobbled it up in an instant. For the girl she left only a little cabbage soup, a hard biscuit, and a bite of roast pork.

The witch climbed back onto her warm spot by the fire. "Now, listen," she said. "When I leave tomorrow you are to clean my house and cook my dinner. Sweep up the yard and do the washing. Then go to my wheat shed. Wild peas are mixed in with the grain. Separate them." The witch turned her face to the wall and in a few minutes was snoring loudly.

Wassilissa crept into a corner of the room. Placing the food before the doll, she began to weep softly. "Here, my little doll, is all of my food. I fear it may not be enough for you to help me this time."

The doll's eyes began to twinkle like stars. It became alive. It ate just a bit and drank just a bit and then spoke to the girl.

"Wassilissa, you are in the witch's house. You are not to fear her, for although she is terrible, she keeps her word. We have only to do as she asks and we shall be fine."

"But ..." began the maiden.

"Eat, my child," interrupted the doll. "Then go to sleep. The morning is wiser than the evening."

In the morning, Wassilissa awoke to the shouts of the Baba Yaga for her gates to unlock. The girl watched the old woman whirl off in the mortar and then thought about all she must do. But when she looked around, she found that it was all done, and the doll was picking the last of the wild peas from the kernels of wheat.

"Now there is only dinner to cook," said the doll.

Wassilissa prepared the old woman's dinner with great care. But she still finished before the horseman in black appeared to signal the beginning of night. At last he came, and behind him came Baba Yaga.

She entered her house. She looked, tapped, and sniffed at everything. She scowled at Wassilissa. "You have done a good job inside and out. But how did you do with my wheat? Mind you, if there is but one pea mixed in, *you* will be my dinner."

"Good evening, Grandmother, and thank you. Please check the wheat. I think it is quite clean."

The witch could not find one pea nor even a grain of sand mixed among the kernels of wheat. Her eyes narrowed. She glared at the young woman then clapped her hands. Three pairs of hands appeared. They began to grind the wheat. "Now bring me my dinner," said the witch. "I am hungry."

Wassilissa put the food before the witch. There was more than the night before. The old woman ate it all except for some borscht—a soup with beets, a crust of bread, and a small piece of beef. She crept up onto her spot by the fire and spoke to Wassilissa.

"Tomorrow do as you did today. Then go into my corn shed. Some of my corn has rotted. If it is not removed, if every kernel is not taken out, it

"Here, my little doll, is all of my food."

will spoil the whole lot. Clean out the corn."

The second day everything happened as it had on the first. When Baba Yaga returned home she found all of the tasks completed. Everything was in perfect order. Baba Yaga poked here and sniffed there. There was not a speck of dust anywhere. The old witch's face became stormy. She clapped for the three pair of hands. They appeared and began to grind the corn. "Bring me my dinner," growled the old woman. "I am very hungry." And she gnashed her teeth.

Wassilissa set the food upon the table and stood silently by while the witch ate. The Baba Yaga eyed her carefully then spoke. "What is the matter with you? You stand there like a dummy. Have you lost your tongue? Surely you have some questions you would like to ask me."

"Well, Grandmother, in truth I have thought of a few."

"Ask them. But remember that not all questions should be asked and that he who knows too much grows old too soon."

"Well, then, I would ask you about the three horsemen—the one dressed in white, the one dressed in red, and the one dressed in black. Who are they?"

"They are my trusted servants. The first is day, the second is the sun, and the third is the night. They will not harm you. Ask me more."

Wassilissa thought of the three pairs of hands. She was about to ask about them but felt a shiver of fear run down her spine. She remained silent.

"Ask me more!" ordered the witch. "Don't you want to know more? Don't you want to know about the hands? Ask me about them!"

"I think not, Grandmother. You yourself said that when one knows too much, one becomes old too soon."

"You were smart," said the witch, "to ask only about what you saw on the outside of this house. If you had asked about the hands they would have carried you off as they did the grain. You would have been ground up for my dinner. Now. I will ask you a question. How is it that you have been able to do what is not humanly possible to do?"

Wassilissa almost told her about the doll but suddenly remembered her mother's warning. "The blessing of my dead mother helps me, Grandmother."

"Is that so?" growled the witch. "Well, I will tell you. I want no one with a blessing on their head under my roof. Get out!" She pushed Wassilissa out the door. She took a skull from the wall and put it on a stick. Shoving it into Wassilissa's hand she said, "Here is the fire your stepmother sent you for. Take it to her. May she have the good of it!"

Wassilissa ran through the forest, the skull lighting the way. By morning she reached the edge of the woods. As day broke, the eyes of the skull stopped glowing.

Wassilissa reached her home and found her stepmother and stepsisters glad to see her. They explained that since she had been gone they could keep no fire burning in the house. They took the skull inside. Its eyes began to glow once more, brighter and brighter and hotter and hotter as it watched the three wherever they went. "Get it out of here!" screamed one of the sisters. "It's going to burn us up!"

But her warning came too late. The skull did what she said it would do and burned the three to ashes.

Wassilissa took the skull and buried it. She closed up the house and moved into town, to the home of an old woman who had no children. She stayed with her through the winter, helping her with all her chores. When spring came she asked the old woman to buy the best thread she could find. "I must keep these hands busy," said Wassilissa. "Let me spin some cloth for you."

The old woman bought the thread. With the help of the doll, Wassilissa spun the most beautiful cloth that had ever been seen. The old woman insisted it be made a gift to the tzar.

The tzar gave it to his tailors to make into shirts, but they would not touch it. They said it was too fine to be cut. The tzar called for the old woman. "Since you wove it, you must know how to sew it," he said to her.

She took the fabric back to Wassilissa, who made a dozen of the finest shirts for the tzar. When he saw them, he commanded that this amazing seamstress be brought before him.

Wassilissa made herself ready. She put on her loveliest gown and dressed her hair. A servant came for her and said His Majesty wished to thank her with his own voice. But when the tzar saw her, he fell in love with her on the spot. He asked her to be his wife. The two were married.

When Wassilissa's father returned from his trip, he learned of all that had happened. He wept with guilt at the cruel treatment his daughter had received. He wept with joy at the good fortune she deserved.

He went to stay with his daughter at the palace. So did the old woman who had grown to love Wassilissa like her own child. And the doll stayed in Wassilissa's pocket until the end of her days.

LIMOUSINE SERVICE PROVIDED

Presenting Information Visually

Baba Yaga is a very famous witch in Russian folklore. But she is very different from the witches within Western fairy tales. She does not live in a gingerbread house or have a big black cauldron and a black cat. She does not wear a black cape or black hat. The way she eats would tell us that she is probably not skinny, either. And finally, she does not ride on a broomstick. She rides in a mortar and steers it with a pestle.

Answer each question. Then draw a mortar and a pestle. Finally, draw an illustration for the story on your own paper. Draw how you imagine Baba Yaga would look arriving at her house in her mortar, steering it with its pestle.

1. What are a mortar and a pestle? How big would a mortar have to be to carry Baba Yaga?

2. What are a mortar and pestle used for? did the American Indians use a mortar and a pestle?

3. What did it look like? How did they make these?

4. Why did they use them?

THE TOOTH FAIRY

Health/Science

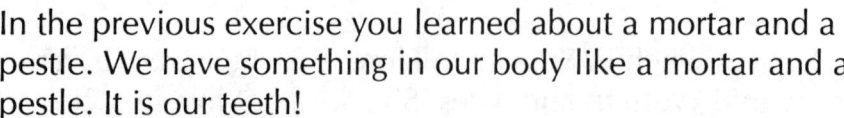

In the previous exercise you learned about a mortar and a pestle. We have something in our body like a mortar and a pestle. It is our teeth!

We have several different types of teeth. This is because different teeth are used for different purposes.

Pay a visit to your family dentist. See if he or she can give you one of each type of our teeth. If not, see if you can get photographs, X-rays, or drawings of our teeth.

Mount your drawings (or the real things). Label each type of tooth and tell what it is used for.

Answer each question.

1. What are teeth made of?
   _____

2. How many teeth does a six-year old child have?
   _____

3. If an adult has all of his or her teeth, how many does he have?
   _____

4. Why is it okay if a six-year old child loses a front tooth?
   _____

5. What holds the tooth in the gum?
   _____

Try this experiment.

As a class, get three real teeth. Examine them carefully. Record color, smoothness, hardness, etc. Put one in a glass of water. Put one in a glass of regular (not diet) cola. Put one in a glass of milk. Add the liquids periodically as they evaporate. Check the teeth every three days for a period of two weeks. Record your observations.

Check for changes in color, smoothness, hardness, etc.

LIVING IN A MATERIAL WORLD

Cultural Geography

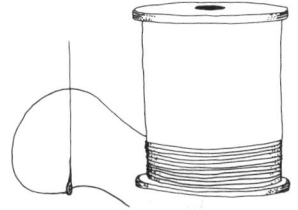

Wassilissa wove thread into a fine fabric. Then she cut the fabric and made shirts for the tzar. What kind of thread did she use? Where did it come from?

Below is a list of fabrics. Research the source of the threads of each fabric. Then tell what type of garment is usually made from that fabric. The first one is done for you.

Fabric	Comes From	Makes
cotton	a plant	shirts, socks
silk		
wool		
linen		
suede		
polyester		
nylon		
rayon		
cashmere		
muslin		
angora		

"MASK"erade

Art

Masquerade balls, Halloween, and costume parties are favorites of children and adults alike. For a little while, we can become something or someone we are not—a beautiful princess or handsome prince; a scary fairy tale witch or skeleton or giant; a cuddly bunny or silly clown.

Did you know that for more than 30,000 years people have been making masks? Before people knew about cloth or clay or paper we used animal skins, feathers, bones, teeth, antlers, plants, and so on. Later we used cloth, clay, plaster, and even gold, silver, and tin. All of these materials—and many more things—are used in mask-making today.

You can make a wonderful mask by using an inflated balloon covered with paper strips soaked in glue or paste.

You will need:
- a balloon
- flour or wheat paste
- water
- newspaper or plastic to work on
- newspaper or tissue paper for covering the balloon

Here are the steps to follow:

1. Blow up your balloon until it is a good size for a mask.
2. Tear or cut your paper into small strips and dip them in the paste. Cover the balloon completely with a layer of the strips.
3. Let this layer dry. Apply three more layers of the paper strips, allowing each layer to dry before applying the next.
4. Let the covered balloon dry completely before you burst it—one or two days.
5. If you want the mask to fit over your head, slice the bottom off. If you want two masks, slice it down the middle from top to bottom.
6. Decorate your mask! What can you make it look like? Paint it, use different scraps of fabric like lace or colorful pieces; use yarn, string, shoelaces, fringed gunny sack material, or wool for hair or a beard, use feathers, beads, buttons, shells, bells, or glitter to complete your character.

WHERE SHE STOPS NOBODY KNOWS

Creative Thinking and Writing

We know that Baba Yaga leaves every morning in her great iron mortar. But where in the world does she go? What in the world is she doing all day long?

Choose either of the activities below.

1. Pretend you are Baba Yaga. You keep a diary about your daily activities. Make entries for every hour on the hour about what you do during the day. For example:

    7:00 A.M. Wake Wassilissa up. Give her impossible chores to do. Call mortar. Open gate.

2. You are Baba Yaga. Write a letter to your sister telling her all the events of your day.

    Dear _____ ,

    _____

    _____

    _____

    _____

    _____

    _____

    _____

    Baba Yaga

THE GHOST, THE KING, AND THE SORCERER

There was once upon a time a certain king. This king was neither old nor ugly; he was not vain or proud; he was not wicked or cruel. His subjects adored him and would show their love by bringing gifts to the palace every day, rain or shine.

Just as the people loved their king, so he loved them. He was honored by all of their gifts, whether large or small. Each and every one found its place in the royal treasury room. So it was that the treasury grew and grew.

The royal Treasurer, however, did not much like the treasury room. He thought it quite an unpleasant place and stayed away from it as much as he could.

"This place stinks," he muttered to himself. "The king thinks he must save every maiden's wishful flower, every old woman's pot of honey, every blacksmith's horseshoe. What a mess! And that ridiculous old beggar priest! That bag of bones brings one fruit every single day. He hasn't missed a day in ten years! Ten years!"

And that was true. For ten years a certain priest had brought the king a different fruit each day. He would offer it in silence, bow with a silent nod of his head, and then disappear silently into the crowd. He had never spoken a word. He had never asked for a thing. And the treasurer had tossed each fruit into a corner in the treasury room.

One day, the king had on his shoulder a pet monkey. The beggar priest arrived and offered his humble gift, one lowly fruit. As the king was about to hand it over to the treasurer, the monkey grabbed it and bit into it. To everyone's surprise, a rare jewel fell to the floor.

"My, my," said the king. "What have we here? I have never seen a pit as this in a peach."

He and the treasurer hurried to the vault. In the corner, buried among the rotting flesh of the fruit, were hundreds of priceless gems!

The following day the beggar again offered the king a piece of fruit. But this time the king refused to take it unless the beggar would speak to him.

"I will speak to you," said the beggar, "but alone."

He and the king went into a private room. The beggar said, "Good king, I have waited ten years for you to be ready to join me on a magical adventure. It may be difficult, and it may be dangerous. But if you have a courageous spirit and we succeed, you will bring great glory to your kingdom. Do you wish to try?"

The king was now very curious. "What must I do?" he asked.

"Tomorrow will be the night of the new moon," said the priest. "Meet me at midnight at the great burial ground at the edge of the city. I will tell you what to do."

The following night was All Soul's Eve. The sky was black, moonless. The great graveyard was lit only by the fires of the grave diggers as they did their ghostly chore. As the king walked the length of the cemetery he heard the moans and cries of the ghosts and goblins which haunted that awful place.

At last the king reached the spot where he was to meet the priest. The priest had arrived before him and was already busy drawing a magic circle on the ground.

"Walk to the hanging yard," ordered the priest. "You will find a corpse hanging from a great tree. Bring it to me."

That was all he said.

The king turned and walked back across the graveyard to the area where criminals were hanged. There indeed was the body of a man hanging from a tree.

The king climbed up into the tree and cut the body down. When it hit the ground it laughed a loud, screeching laugh. The king was startled, but asked, "What is so funny?" The moment the words left his lips, the body flew back up into the tree. The king knew he was in the company of a ghost, and that the ghost would not willingly let him take the body to the priest.

He climbed the tree again and cut the corpse down again. He put the body upon his back and began trudging across the cemetery—this time without speaking a word.

"My, my," said the king. "What have we here?"

"Do you like riddles?" the ghost asked suddenly. "I will make your walk more pleasant. I will ask you some riddles."

The king did not reply.

"Well, then, here is the first. A king's son and his faithful servant were out hunting. They became separated from the rest of the hunting party. After a time they came to a lake. On the far side of the lake they saw some young maidens at play in the water. One of the maidens was beautiful beyond words. She caught the prince's eye. She knew a certain sign language, a way of talking with her hands. Using her hands, she told the prince that she was a princess. She told him where her father's palace was, how he could get there, and how they could meet in secret that very night. And then she told him that she loved him.

But the prince understood none of this. He did not know this language of the hands and thought that the maiden was behaving a bit oddly. His servant, however, understood all that had been said. He explained the princess's message to his master. That night, the prince made his way to the secret spot arranged by the princess. The two fell in love and planned to elope, to run away and marry secretly.

'But,' said the princess, 'I must ask one small proof of your love for me,'

'Name it,' answered the prince. 'It shall be done.'

'I do not trust your manservant,' said the princess. 'One person should not know so much about your business. He could cause problems for us.'

A voice in the darkness cried out. 'Never, my lady! Never! Never will I betray my master! And never will I allow you to sentence me to death!'

The prince's servant rushed out from where he had been hiding. He had followed in secret. He had guessed the princess's fears and knew what she would want his master to do.

'Hold her fast!' said the servant. 'We will take her from this place this very night!'

They did just that. They carried her away to the prince's kingdom and she was wed to the prince.

But the princess's aging parents never knew what had become of their daughter. In a short time, they died of grief."

The ghost chuckled. "Now," it said, "who was responsible for the death of the girl's parents? Who was to blame? Was it the prince, the princess, the manservant, or someone else? If you know the answer, you must give it. If you can answer and do not, your head will explode."

End of Part I

TUTTI-FRUTTI

Science

In the story, a priest brought a fruit to the king every day for ten years. How many fruits did he bring? (Don't forget to add one extra day every fourth year.)

We all know what fruits are. We have eaten many different kinds of fruits and can name many. But did you know that deciding what is a fruit and what is not is trickier than it seems?

Some fruits *have* seeds, some fruits *are* seeds, and some fruits are the mature (ripe) flowers of plants.

Place each fruit in the correct column. You may work in groups. Remember! If you have trouble, look in an encyclopedia or talk to your reference librarian.

apple	pineapple	olive	papaya	coconut	strawberry
grape	avocado	mango	almond	blackberry	cherry
mulberry	orange	Brazil nut	pomegranate	cashew	
banana	peach	Macadamia	raspberry	plum	lemon
apricot		kiwi			

Has Seeds   **Is a Seed**   **Is a Flower**

_____ _____ _____
_____ _____ _____
_____ _____ _____
_____ _____ _____
_____ _____ _____
_____ _____ _____
_____ _____ _____
_____ _____ _____

MORE TUTTI-FRUTTI

Presenting Information Visually

Illustrate each of the fruits on the previous page. Make each fruit its actual-size. Color it accurately. You may wish to illustrate the fruit in two ways, for example: whole, and cut open to reveal the seed, pit, or stone if there is one.

Research in groups some basic information about the fruit. Then, on your own, explain where it grows, whether it grows on a tree or bush, what the texture is like, and so on.

ALL THAT GLITTERS IS NOT GOLD

Gemology

In the story, the king makes an astonishing discovery. Each fruit that the priest had given him contained a precious jewel!

Complete the table for each of the gemstones given below. You may use an encyclopedia.

Name of Stone	Color of Stone	Countries Where Found	Birthstone Month
Diamond			
Emerald			
Ruby			
Sapphire			
Aquamarine			
Amethyst			
Citrine			
Topaz			
Garnet			
Jade			
Opal			
Tourmaline			
Peridot			
Pearl			
Turquoise			

MORE OF THE SAME

Working with Synonyms and Antonyms

We know that synonyms are words that have the same or nearly the same meaning as another word. *Antonyms* are words that have the opposite meaning.

For each word from the story, write as many synonyms and antonyms as you can.

OLD
  same _____

  opposite _____

UGLY
  same _____

  opposite _____

ADORED
  same _____

  opposite _____

GIFTS
  same _____

  opposite _____

LARGE
  same _____

  opposite _____

SMALL
  same _____

  opposite _____ _____

ORDER IN THE COURT

Building Classification Skills

The Royal Treasurer did not like the Royal Treasury Room because it was in such a mess! Besides all the fruit, here are some of the things that were in it:

coins	hairbrushes	pots of honey	bows and arrows
bread	vases	a Nintendo	fish in fishbowls
quill pens	a harp	necklaces	an electronic calculator
rubies	salt	paintings	paint brushes
rings	daffodils	parrots	a computer
a sundial	sugar	shields	a wristwatch
cinnamon	a spear	puppies	soft blankets
swords	horseshoes	an hourglass	colored chalk
a flute	a bridle	paprika	lace handkerchiefs
pepper	diamonds	orchids	a mandolin
emeralds	ink	tea	down pillows
reins	scabbards	canaries	a chess set
robes	tapestries	salt	paint brushes
paints	roses	bubble bath	baked hams
combs	a radio	bracelets	embroidered towels
daggars	cats	stirrups	aquamarines
a lute	a saddle	daggers	a CD player
hats	smoked fish	silk sheets	silk shirts
poems	potatoes	perfume	velvet capes

It is your job to get this room in order. On your own paper, sort all of the items into logical categories. Write what things will go into each category.

There are several things in the Treasury Room that do not belong there at all. List them and tell why they do not belong.

THE GHOST, THE KING, AND THE SORCERER, PART II

he king was in a predicament, a very bad spot. He was quite sure he knew the answer to the riddle. He guessed that if he spoke, the corpse would fly back to the tree. But if he did not speak, his head would explode. And he was not too pleased about that happening. So he spoke:

"The girl's own father is responsible. He was the king of that country. It is the king's job to see all and know all that is happening in his kingdom. He did not even guard his own daughter well. He was not aware of the strangers in his land. He alone is guilty."

"Well spoken!" said the ghost, and it flew with the body back into the tree.

Once again the king was forced to turn back, to make the long walk across the huge graveyard. For the third time, he cut down the corpse, shouldered the heavy burden, and started off in the direction of the priest.

It was not long before the ghost spoke again. "You seem to be good at problems. Here is another one for you."

Now, the king did *not* want to hear another riddle. He knew that the ghost would command him to answer it or have his head explode. But he could not protest, he could not refuse, for if he spoke the corpse would return to the tree! What was he to do? He could only hope for the riddle he could not solve.

"Here is a good one," said the ghost. "See how you like it. A merchant was traveling in a distant land. He came to a crossroads and did not know which way to go. On one side of the road was a richly dressed man. By his appearance the merchant thought he might even be a nobleman. On the other side of the road was a man who was dirty and dressed in rags. The merchant approached the rich man and asked for directions. The rich man answered that he could not help, that he too was lost. He said also that he had just been robbed and needed just a little money to help him get to the next town. The merchant approached the poor man. The poor man told a sad tale of hunger and cold and asked for money. But he could not tell the merchant which road to take for he too was a stranger in those parts. The merchant had one gold coin which he could give. What should he do? Should he give either man money or neither? What is your answer? If you have one and do not give it your head will explode."

The king had an answer and so gave it. The ghost and the corpse soared away to the tree.

And so it went all night long. Back and forth, to and fro, riddle and answer, problem and solution. But through it all, the king stayed cheerful. He did not stop to rest; he did not grumble or complain. The black sky of night began to fade into the gray of dawn and still the ghost quizzed on.

"Hear, o gracious king, this puzzling tale. A widowed king and his son (who was a young man himself, you must know), were on a long journey in the dead of winter. They came upon two sets of footprints in the snow. Both men were skilled trackers, and they could tell that the footprints belonged to two women. They examined the size of the step and the make of the boot. They guessed that the women were of a noble family—possibly even and queen and her daughter. The mother would be the owner of the larger, sturdier footprints and the daughter would be the owner of the smaller, more delicate set of footprints.

Now, for many years the prince had wished that his father would remarry, but the king would not. The prince did not want to place his own happiness before his father's, and so he, too, had not married. In these footprints he saw a stroke of luck. He proposed a contract. 'We will find the owners of these footprints,' he said to his father. 'If they turn out to be a queen and her daughter, and if they both are unmarried, we will marry them. You will marry the owner of the larger footprints, and I will marry the owner of the smaller footprints.' The king thought there was little chance of this happening, so he agreed. The two made a solemn promise.

They hurried along the trail. At last they came upon the two women—the makers of the footprints. They were, in fact, a queen and her daughter. They were fleeing their country where there had been a war and the king (the queen's husband, that is) had been killed. So both were unmarried!

Well! The king (the prince's father, that is) knew he was stuck. He had made a promise, and he knew he would have to keep it. There was just one

"The king walked along in silence, thinking about the riddle."

small problem. The mother was the owner of the smaller footprints and the daughter was the owner of the larger ones! So according to their oath, the son would have to marry the queen, the father would marry the princess. And so it was. A year later a son was born to each woman."

The ghost in the corpse again chuckled. "Now," it said, "exactly how were these two babies related to each other? Answer if you can, or your head will explode."

The king walked along in silence, thinking about the riddle. He thought and he thought, but could not come up with an answer. Up ahead, the priest could be seen, finishing his preparations for whatever ceremony was to take place.

The ghost again spoke. "Your majesty," it said, "we have little time. Listen to me carefully if you value your life. You have proved yourself to be a great king. But all will end if you do not follow my instructions. The priest is no priest, but an evil sorcerer. He rules this cemetery and keeps us from our eternal rest. Now he would have your kingdom as well. When you deliver me to him, he will place me on a throne inside his magic circle. He will say some magic spells. Then he will tell you to bow down to me and worship me. You must not do it. You must say, 'I do not know the right way to bow. I have never had to do it. Please show me the proper way.' The sorcerer will kneel down. When he is not looking, you must take your sword and strike him dead."

The king nodded his understanding.

They reached the magician, who smiled a crafty smile. He took the king's burden and placed it on a throne inside the magic circle. He said magic spells. Then he told the king to bow down.

"Sir," said the king, "being a king, I have not had much experience in bowing. This must be done correctly. Can you show me the proper way?"

The magician grumbled, but knelt down on the ground. With a mighty blow of his sword, the king cut off the sorcerer's head.

From all around there rose a cry of great joy. The spell had been broken. The souls were freed.

"Your majesty," said the ghost, "when you began this adventure, you did not know what was at stake. You suffered a hard night. You could have stopped at any time, but you did not. Tonight you played the game of life. Your goodness won the game for all of us. Ask a reward. It shall be yours."

The king thought, and then smiled. "I ask this: Let the tales you have told me throughout the night spread until they have reached the four corners of the earth. In these riddles are the answers to all life's questions. In these tales are the lessons for living. Now. Godspeed. Rest in peace."

RIDDLE ME THIS

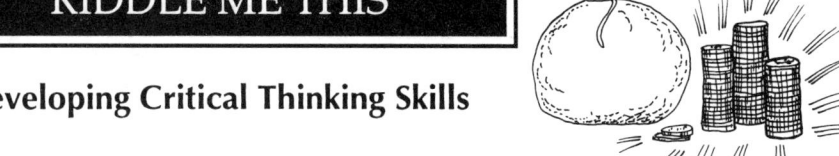

Developing Critical Thinking Skills

In the story, the ghost asks the king a riddle about a merchant at a crossroads. The king has an answer, but the story does not say what it is. What would your answer be? Write what you think and explain your reasons.

_____
_____
_____
_____
_____
_____
_____
_____

The ghost also asks the king about how the two babies are related. The king cannot give an answer. Can you? Think carefully. The question is not how the fathers and mothers are related to each child but how the two children are related. Work with a partner or in a team. Draw a diagram if that helps. Do we have a word in our language describing how they are related?

_____
_____
_____
_____
_____
_____
_____
_____

BRAINBUSTERS

More Critical Thinking

The ghost riddled the king all night long. He gave him problems to solve that do not have clear or easy answers.

Here are some questions that the ghost could have asked the king. They were not in the story.

Divide the class into teams. Discuss each question. As a team, come up with one answer for each question. Then discuss your answers with the class. Be ready to tell why you answered the way you did.

1. A certain chief of India made a journey to a distant land. There he met a beautiful maiden and fell in love with her. He wanted to marry her, but his tribe would not allow the chief to marry anyone who was not a member of that tribe. He must make a decision. Should he marry and give up his rule, his family, his friends, and his homeland, or should he marry his true love?

2. A sorcerer offered a poor man riches and happiness for his family. But in exchange, the man would become horribly ugly. The man had a wife and children. What should he do?

3. A prince was to marry a beautiful princess. The night before their wedding she fell off a balcony and broke her neck. This left her paralyzed. Should the prince back out of the marriage or not?

4. Two brothers were simple farmers. One day, one said he must go to town to buy seed for planting. The other said, "While you are there, please see if they have an ointment, a special medicine for the blisters on my hands. I will pay you when you get back." The first brother went to town. He bought the seed and found the medicine for his brother. But the medicine was very expensive. The two had not talked about price, but the first brother bought the medicine because he knew his brother wanted it. When he got back, the second brother said, "That medicine cost too much! How can you expect me to pay?" What solution did they reach?

WHO'S ON FIRST?

Deductive Reasoning

Here is another riddle. It seems very difficult but really is not once you know how to solve it.

From the facts, figure out the names of the players playing the different positions on the baseball team.

Andy does not like the catcher. Ed's sister is going to marry the second baseman. The man who plays center field is taller than the man who plays right field. Jose and the third baseman live in the same building. Paul, Carlos, and the pitcher each won $5.00 on a lottery ticket. Ed and the outfielders play soccer in their free time. The pitcher's wife is the third baseman's sister. Carlos, Jose, and Andy are either the pitcher, catcher, first baseman, second baseman, third baseman, or shortstop. They are taller than Sam. The other infielders are shorter than Sam. Paul, Andy, and the shortstop went for pizza after the last game. Paul, Jose, Bill, and the catcher were beaten by the second baseman in homeruns hit. Sam raises chickens. The catcher and the third baseman each have two children. Ed, Paul, Jerry, the rightfielder and the center fielder are bachelors. The others are married. The shortstop, the third baseman, and Bill each bought new cars last year. One of the outfielders is either Mike or Andy. Jerry is taller than Bill. Each of them is heavier than the third baseman. Mike is shorter than Bill. Sam and the pitcher play cards with the first and second baseman. Bill likes the shortstop's car. Carlos and the third baseman went to the movies with Jose, Sam, and Ed. Jose and the first baseman went to the left fielder's house for Thanksgiving. Sam lost the right fielder's glove. Jerry, Andy, and the outfielders play musical instruments. The pitcher paints.

This is how you solve the problem. Make a table to organize your information.

	Pitcher	Catcher	1st	2nd	3rd	SS	LF	RF	CF
Andy		N							
Ed				N					
Jose					N				
Paul	N								
Carlos	N								
Sam									
Bill									
Jerry									
Mike									

Complete the table with Y for *yes* and N for *no* for the things you know or can figure out. The table has been started for you. For example, if Andy does not like the catcher, then he cannot be the catcher. Ed is not the second baseman, and so on.

BABY TALK

Popular Riddles

There are many popular riddles in the English language. They have been told to children for years and years. Here are some of them. See if you can figure out the answers. Then make some riddles of your own. Or, if you speak another language, tell riddles from your native language.

1. What has four wheels and flies?
2. What gets wetter and wetter the more it dries?
3. What has legs but cannot walk?
4. What has a head but cannot talk?
5. What has eyes but cannot see?
6. What lives in a school but doesn't learn?
7. What keeps on running but never moves?
8. What always holds its hands in front of its face?
9. What do you lose every time you stand up?
10. What can go up the chimney down but can't go down the chimney up?
11. What animal goes on four legs in the morning, two at noon, and three in the evening?
12. As I was going to St. Ives
    I met a man with seven wives.
    Every wife had seven sacks,
    Every sack had seven cats,
    Every cat had seven kits.
    Kits, cats, sacks, and wives,
    How many were going to St. Ives?
13. Little Nancy Etticoat
    Wears a white petticoat
    And has a little red nose.
    The longer she stands
    The shorter she grows.
    What is she?
14. Thirty-two white horses
    Standing on a red hill.
    First they stomp
    Then they chomp
    Then they stand still.
    What are they?

INTERNATIONAL DELHI

Geography

The story you just read comes from India. Here is a map of India and the countries that border it. Label the countries. Locate the capital of India. Find the three major bodies of water that border the country and put those on the map.

CAP O' RUSHES

here was once a king who had three daughters. One day, having nothing better to do, he began to wonder whether or not his daughters really loved him.
He called the eldest daughter into his chambers. "My dear," he began, "the day will come when this old head will fall like ripe fruit. I should like to know, before that sad day comes, how much you love me."

The girl put her arms around her father's neck and kissed him gently upon the cheek. "Silly goose," she laughed, "what questions you do ask! Why, I love you so much that my love cannot be measured. I love you wider than the oceans are wide. I love you more deeply than the oceans are deep."

The king stroked his daughter's hair. "You do love me. I can see that."

He called in his second daugher. "My dear, in time these eyes will close in an endless sleep. Before the day comes when I can no longer behold your sweet face, tell me, how much do you love me?"

The princess sat upon her father's lap and patted his hand. "Oh, father, do not sadden me with such talk. How could you question my love for you? It is vaster than the skies above, brighter than the brightest star."

The king held his daughter's hand in his own. "You do love me. I can see that."

Finally he called in his youngest daughter. She sat, as was her way, at his feet. "My child," he said, "before these ears become as stones, before I can no longer hear the music of your voice, pray tell me, do you love me?"

"Why, father, what a silly question. Of course I do."

"Well, how much?" asked the king.

"Why, as much as fresh meat loves salt!"

"What?" bellowed the king. "As much as fresh meat loves salt? I am nothing more to you than a slab of meat? You do not love me at all! Get out of my sight! Leave this house at once! It is your home no longer!"

The king had risen to his feet and was shaking his fist at the girl. She backed away, sobbing, then turned and ran from the palace.

She ran throughout the day and into the night. She ran into the face of the rising sun. She ran until her legs, weak and trembling, could hold her up no longer. She fell and slept.

When she awoke, she found herself at the edge of a stream. All around the stream were cattails and marsh grasses and rushes. The princess began to pick the sharp-edged leaves of the rushes. They stung and tore the flesh of her hands, but she did not stop. When she had enough, she wove the rushes into a sort of cape that had a hood. With this she covered her royal gown and started off.

How far or how long she traveled is too long for the telling in this tale. But at last she reached the palace of a distant kingdom. She went up to the sentry at the gate. The soldier stood straight and tall, proud of his job for the king.

"What do ya' want?" he snarled at the girl. "State yer business at once er be off!"

"I am looking for work," said the princess (who looked nothing at all like a princess at the moment).

"We have no work for beggars here," answered the guard. "That is, unless ya' would not mind being a dish washer. There's always plenty o' dishes to scrape and pots to scrub around here. They'll work yer fingers to the bone, they will!"

"I will do anything," answered the princess.

"Humph! The likes o' ya' doesn't look like it's done an honest day's work in its life. But we'll gi' ya the chance."

The sentry called for a messenger, who led the princess to the palace kitchen.

The chief cook, an old woman with a very greasy apron and a wodden spoon in her hand, eyed the girl up and down. "Well, ya'r young enough to have strength for the job. But yer hands don't look like they've done a lick o' work in all their days. Who be ye, anyway? Where do ya' hail from? What be yer name?"

"I have no home. I am just a wanderer. I have no name. I could use something to eat, but I'll work hard for it, I promise you."

When she awoke, she found herself at the edge of a stream.

"Ya' talk all lady-like," said the cook. "Methinks ya' ha' some secret to keep. But we've all got a right to our secrets, providin' no harm's done. Ya' got no name, then? Well, I'll be callin' ya' Cap o'Rushes."

She led Cap o'Rushes to a wooden table. "Sit yerself down and eat a bite. Over there's where ya'll sleep. There's pots in the sink. I expect them to shine like silver."

And so Cap o'Rushes stayed on. She washed pots and scrubbed floors. She slept on a mat in a room no bigger than a broom closet.

One day, all the servants were a-buzz with chitter and chatter. "Did ya' hear?" they all exclaimed. "Tonight there will be a grand ball! The prince is lookin' for a bride! And we may watch the dance from the sides, if we ha' finished our chores. Will ya' be goin', Cap o'Rushes?"

"Well, I don't know," she answered. "I have so very much work to do, you know. And I get so very tired. We shall see."

When evening came, Cap o'Rushes said she was too tired to go. She pretended to go to her bed. But as soon as all of the servants were out of sight, she threw off her grassy cape, tidied herself (just as a princess knows how to do), and hurried off to the ball.

Cap o'Rushes was the last to enter the great ballroom. When she walked in, a hush fell over the corwd. All eyes were upon her. None was so beautiful, so splendidly dressed. The prince went up to her and led her to the floor. She danced like an angel, and the prince was in love. He would not leave her side.

But our princess made the excuse that there was a guest she must talk to. "I'll only be a moment," she said. But she slipped off into the crowd and did not return.

In the morning the servants tittled with excitement. "Oh, Cap o'Rushes! Ya' should ha' seen the sight! A great lady arrived, more beautiful than day. The prince would not leave her side. But she disappeared before the dance was done, an' the prince is beside himself with worry that he'll never see the lady again. Why he's havin' another ball tonight, in hopes that she'll come again. Will ya' go Cap o'Rushes?"

"Well, I don't know. I have so very much work to do, and I get so very tired. ..."

The second night happened as the first. The princess was the last to arrive and the first to leave, slipping away unnoticed before the ball was over. The whole palace was whispering about the mysterious lady.

A third ball was planned. Cap o'Rushes went as before. The prince would dance with no one else. But try as he might, he could find out nothing about her—not her country, not her home, not even her name. "Though you will not declare your love for me, I will declare my love for you." He took a golden ring from his finger and gave it to this mysterious maiden—a princess who was a dish washer in his own palace. "If you accept this, I know you love me and will return to me."

Cap o'Rushes took the ring, but said nothing. She excused herself—"just for a moment"—saying she must get some air, she felt quite faint. Then she disappeared as she had done on the nights before.

End of Part I

METAPHORS A TO Z

Using Metaphors

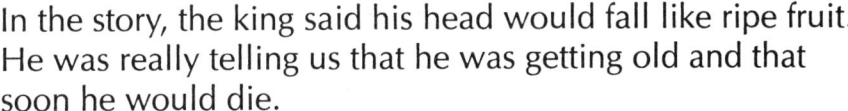

In the story, the king said his head would fall like ripe fruit. He was really telling us that he was getting old and that soon he would die.
When we compare two things that are not at all alike we are using metaphors.

Read each metaphor.

To be an angel means to be a very helpful person.
To get off someone's back means to stop bothering her.
If a person is a *cold fish*, he does not show much emotion.
If a person *moves heaven and earth*, she does—or tries to do—something difficult or impossible.
If a person's *eyes are glued* to something, he is staring at it.
If a person is *skating on thin ice,* he is acting foolishly or not thinking about possible dangers or bad consequences.
If a person says she is going to *turn over a new leaf*, she means she is going to try to do or be better.
If a person *weaves a tangled web*, she tells a lot of lies.

Write a sentence for each metaphor given above. One has been done for you.

1. Thank you for being such an angel helping me with my homework.

2. _____

3. _____

4. _____

5. _____

_____

6. _____

_____

7. _____

_____

8. _____

_____

APOSTROPHE CATASTROPHE

Working with Apostrophes

In our language, an apostrophe (') can be used for several different purposes. It can show that something belongs to someone: *Sally's horse*. It can be used to make contractions—to make two little words into one: *do not = don't*. It can be used to mean more than one for a letter, a number, or a figure: *Three s's; two 4's; five ^'s*. Or it can be used to show that letters of a word have been left out.

In our story, when the palace guard, the cook, and the servants talk, the words do not look quite right, and you see a lot of apostrophes. This is because those characters speak with an accent. Their words are written in a way to help you pronounce them as the characters would have, to use their accent.

Start with the sentry's line, "What do ya' want?" he snarled at the girl, and stop with the cook's line, "What be yer name?" Rewrite the lines so the words and grammar are in standard English. The first line is done for you.

"What do you want," he snarled at the girl. "State your business at once or be off!"

MORE APOSTROPHES

Working with Apostrophes: Contractions

Apostrophes are used to make two words into one. These are called *contractions*. To make a contraction, one or more letters is taken out of one of the words. An apostrophe is put in to show where the letters were.

Write the two words that each contraction stands for. Some have been done for you. These will give you a clue about how to do others like them.

I'm	I am	aren't	are not
I'll	I will	isn't	
I'd	I would	wasn't	
I've	I have	weren't	
you're	you are	can't	
you'll		don't	
you'd		doesn't	
you've		didn't	
he's	he is or he has	haven't	
he'll		hasn't	
he'd		hadn't	
she's		couldn't	
she'll		wouldn't	
she'd		shouldn't	
we're		mustn't	
we'll		let's	let us
we'd		here's	here is
we've		where's	

A MAN'S HOME IS HIS CASTLE

Presenting Information Visually

Many of the stories in this book have a castle or a palace. A castle is not just a beautiful home for a king. It is built in a way to protect him, his family, his servants, and even his knights or soldiers.

Choose one of the following projects:

1. Draw a castle. Find out about castles of Europe. You can find many pictures. Find out how they were made, their main parts. Include in your drawing a moat, the drawbridge, a courtyard, parapets, turrets, and towers, and of course, the dungeon. (Look in an encyclopedia or dictionary if you don't know what these parts are.

2. Work with a team. Make a castle using Legos, clay, or any material you can think of. Include your family in the project. What ideas do they have for materials for a castle?

3. Do you live near the beach? Make a sand castle. Photograph it.

4. Make a book of the castles of Europe. Make photocopies of the castle, then write where it was built, when it was built, what it was named, who lived there, and any other interesting information you can find.

WHEN IRISH EYES ARE SMILING

Geography

The story of Cap o'Rushes is an old story from Ireland. Where is Ireland?

Draw a map of Ireland. You may trace it or draw it freehand. Draw the countries that border Ireland. Name them. Draw important bodies of water that border Ireland.

CAP O' RUSHES, PART II

fter that, there were no more balls. Several weeks went by, and no news was learned about the lady. A gloominess seemed to fill the air. The servants worked in silence. Children playing in the courtyard were hushed by their parents. The prince took to his bed and could not be cheered. The king and queen fretted when doctors could give no cure.

Cap o'Rushes watched the old cook as she stood stirring a pot of soup. Tears rolled down the old woman's cheeks.

Cap o'Rushes put her arms around the old woman's shoulders. "Why are you crying?" she asked.

"Oh, milady—for tho' ya' will not say, I know ya' are a lady—our prince is dying for love o' the mysterious maiden. An' I think it's a mean trick she has played wi' his heart, to make him love her and then leave."

"Perhaps in the past," said Cap o'Rushes, "this maiden was deeply hurt by a man she loved. Perhaps she is afraid to trust to love again."

The old cook eyed Cap o'Rushes narrowly. "'Perhaps' and 'the Past,'" she said, "are the Land o' the Lost. 'Tomorrow' is the Land o' the Fool. These eyes o' mine may be old, Cap o'Rushes, but they still see a thing or two."

She handed her scullery maid the spoon. "Here, girl. You finish stirrin' the soup. I'll rest my bones a bit."

Cap o'Rushes took the spoon. She thought and thought as she stirred and stirred. She ladled some of the soup into a tureen, a special bowl she

"How did this ring get into my soup?" asked the prince.

knew only the prince used. She looked at the cook. The old woman seemed to be asleep. Cap o'Rushes reached into her apron pocket and drew out the golden ring. She dropped it into the bowl. Calling a servant she said, "The cook made this especially for the prince. It's an old recipe, an old home remedy. It will help him. Take it to him at once."

The prince drank the soup. When he saw the ring at the bottom of the bowl, he cried out. "Who made this soup? Bring me the person who made me this soup at once!"

The cook was led to the prince's room. He looked at her and said, "You did not make this soup. Who did?"

"Well, I made it," she said, "but my dish washer stirred it."

"Bring her to me," ordered the prince.

So Cap o'Rushes came.

"How did this ring get into my soup?" asked the prince.

"I put it there," she answered.

"Where did you get it?"

"From the man I love."

And Cap o'Rushes removed her grassy cape and let it fall to the floor. Standing before the prince was the maiden from the ball.

The prince was soon well, and a wedding was planned. Kings and queens and noblemen from far and wide were invited. Before the wedding feast was prepared, Cap o'Rushes went to the old cook.

"I want every dish prepared without so much as a grain of salt," she said.

"That will be a nasty trick," said the cook.

"It's for a reason," said the princess.

"So be it," said the cook.

The prince and princess were wed and all of the guests sat down to a huge feast. But before long the guests began to grumble about the food.

Suddenly, at one of the tables, an invited king burst into tears. When asked what was the matter he said, "I once had a daughter. I asked her how much she loved me and she said, 'As much as fresh meat loves salt.' I was angry. I thought she had insulted me. I sent her away. I thought she hated me. Only after eating this food without salt do I see that she truly loved me best of all. And she may be dead, for all I know."

Cap o'Rushes stood up. "Look, Father. Who do you see?" She went to her father and put her arms around his neck.

And after that, everyone in this story lived happily ever after.

MINE, YOURS, AND OURS

Associations

Following is a list of characters from the story. In the box is a list of objects or traits. Match each object with one or more of the characters who could have had it or used it.

a greasy apron	a castle	a uniform	potions pride
three daughters	a grassy cape	brooms	wooden spoons
fans	a golden ring	a throne	a club
a treasury room	pretty gowns	mops	a spatula
a grey beard	a cape	a joker	robe
a short temper	wrinkles	a sword	dancing shoes
a wounded heart	pots and pans	servants	an accent
a disguise	soap	dust rags	a prince's love
a crown	soldiers	a queen	jealous feelings
a powdered wig	patients	jewelry	bags of herbs
a foolish father	buckets	a carving knife	chores
a ruffled shirt	a washboad	a mortar and a pestle	a sceptre
a rug beater	a paring knife	sore and cut fingers	eggs
a cat o' nine tails	a joker	a scarf to cover the hair	a plumed hat

Cap o'Rushes' Father
_____
_____

The Palace Guard
_____
_____

The Cook
_____
_____

The Royal Housekeepers
_____
_____

Doctors
_____
_____

Women at the Ball
_____
_____

The Prince
_____
_____

Cap o'Rushes
_____
_____

AS MUCH AS FRESH MEAT LOVES SALT

Spelling and Vocabulary

In the gameboard are words from the story and many, many other words. There are at least 162 words. How many can you find?

To make words, connect adjoining letters. The letters can be side by side, up and down, down and up, backwards, or diagonal. The only requirements are that the letters must touch, you can not skip letters, and the same letter cannot be used twice in the same word. For example, GOING is not allowable, because G would have to be used twice. RUSHES has been done for you. HAPPY HUNTING!

O	F	R→	U	H	S
R	O	M	E	S	E
B	H	C	E	T	A
A	N	V	A	L	W
D	I	G	O	N	I
P	R	O	S	E	R

IT MAKES A BIG DIFFERENCE

Working with Antonyms

For each sentence from the story, replace the underlined word with an antonym, or a word that has the opposite meaning. Then rewrite the sentence.

1. There was once a king who had three daughters.

2. She ran throughout the day and into the night.

3. At last she reached the palace of a distant kingdom.

4. The soldier stood straight and tall.

5. Tonight there will be a grand ball.

6. The prince is looking for a bride.

7. Cap o'Rushes was the last to enter the great ballroom.

8. The old woman seemed to be asleep.

9. It's an old recipe.

10. Standing before the prince was the maiden from the ball.

RING SOUP

Sensible Answers/Building Vocabulary

In the story, the prince found a ring at the bottom of his bowl of soup. That is not something that is likely to be found in the soup you eat!

Work with a partner. You are making "Math Soup." What would you add? What would you leave out? The first few are done for you.

Add	Leave out
a calculator	a dictionary
multiplication tables	

Now you are preparing "Computer Soup." What would you add? What would you leave out? The first few are done for you.

Add	Leave out
a user's manual	
lots of ideas	

PICTURE THIS

Demonstrating Comprehension through Illustration

Following are some phrases or sentences from the story. Choose one and illustrate it on your own paper. When everyone's illustrations are complete, display them in the order in which they occurred in the story.

the king's bed chambers

silly goose

The princess sat upon her father's lap.

Leave this house at once!

She backed away, sobbing.

She ran into the face of the sun.

She found herself at the edge of a stream.

All around the stream were cattails.

She wove the rushes into a sort of cape.

the sentry at the gate

a scullery maid

the chief cook, an old woman with a very greasy apron and a wooden spoon

There are pots in the sink.

She slept on a mat in a room no bigger than a broom closet.

When she walked in, a hush fell over the crowd.

She danced like an angel.

She ladled some of the soup into a tureen.

The old woman seemed to be asleep.

An invited king burst into tears.

She put her arms around his neck.